SOME EARLY MASSACHUSETTS

Broadsides

D1510310

A Massachusetts Historical Society Picture Book

BOSTON: 1964

COPYRIGHT 1964
BY THE MASSACHUSETTS HISTORICAL SOCIETY

Other PICTURE BOOKS in this series are still in print and may be had at the prices indicated from the publisher, the Massachusetts Historical Society, 1154 Boylston Street, Boston 15, Massachusetts. When ordering by mail, please add an extra ten cents for postage on each item desired. All prices subject to change without notice.

COMPOSITION BY THE ANTHOENSEN PRESS, PORTLAND, MAINE
PRINTED BY THE MERIDEN GRAVURE COMPANY, MERIDEN, CONNECTICUT

Foreword

BROADSIDES—those newssheets usually printed on one side and intended to be posted on a wall or read and thrown away—were for our first two centuries the chief medium of communication between the range of the human voice and the printed pamphlet. They served the function of the modern radio, television, and, to a great extent, the newspaper.

Although these sheets flew from the colonial printing presses like autumn leaves before a wind, very few of those printed have survived. Unlike books and pamphlets, they were for the moment, sparks and flashes of news. When their news was cool, their blank sides invited the quill of anyone with a note to write. Many survive only because that note was regarded as important long after the printed news was old. Others became wrapping paper, lining for hats and pie plates, and even stiffening for the squares in patchwork quilts. The series here reproduced ends appropriately with the Declaration of Independence (No. 29), and should begin with The Oath of a Freeman, but no copy of that first product of the Cambridge Press has survived.

In all states at that time, the governments communicated with the governed by broadside printings of executive proclamations (No. 20), of which the 1665 Conditions for New-Planters in New York is typical (No. 3). In Massachusetts, where the government was usually under popular control, these proclamations are less important as executive orders than as official statements of news. Thus those of 1675 and 1676 deal with King Philip's War (Nos. 4 and

5). The two Andros proclamations (Nos. 6 and 7) represent the Colony's brief experience with arbitrary executive government, and are answered by the popular verse hailing the Prince of Orange (No. 8). The Relation of Captain Bull, Concerning the Mohawks (No. 9) illustrates the vigorous action of the restored popular governments.

These proclamations are full of social history. That of Thomas Povey dealing with John Quelch (No. 11) relates to pirates, and that of Dummer for the arrest of Henry Phillips (No. 14) is the horrified reaction to a duel on Boston Common. The unofficial Speech of Joseph T-sd-le in the House of Representatives (No. 25) deals with another social problem of the moment, the theater. The two longest series are the Thanksgiving and Fast day proclamations, which often recount the reasons why the people should give thanks or mourn.

The Massachusetts Puritans were alone among their contemporaries in thinking that the people should be informed of all legislation, and provided for it by law, setting up the Cambridge Press in a defiance of Parliamentary statute as serious as a defiance in the coining of pine tree shillings. In Bay Colony days the members of the legislature carried home at the end of each session broadside printings of the laws to be exhibited at town meeting.

The town of Boston similarly communicated with its inhabitants on such matters as naming Streets, Lanes & Alleys (No. 12), and dealing with smallpox (No. 16). The Trueborn Sons of Liberty followed the same practice (No. 24), and the popular party spread their versions of such events as the massacre of The Fifth of March (No. 26) in the same way. In this series, the unofficial List of the Names of the Provincials killed at Concord (No. 27), and the like, merge with the proclamations (No. 28) and finally the legislation of the Watertown Congress as it gradually became a government.

The colleges also communicated with the public by means of broadsides. The triennial catalogues of graduates were the Who's Whos of the colonial period, providing a list of the clergymen and the majority of holders of important civil office. Each new Triennial was read with interest to see who was starred as dead, and to see in the new classes the names of the rising generation of leaders. The Theses sheets, of which we reproduce that for 1643 (No. 1), give the names of the new Bachelors, and the Quaestiones, the names of the new Masters of Arts, both carrying the list of topics which the new graduates were prepared to argue. These were regarded as proof of the intellectual maturity of the colonies. The news of the burning of Harvard Hall (No. 21) was thus of great popular concern.

Of the many unofficial newssheets issued by the printers in the eighteenth century, perhaps the most popular were the accounts of hangings, like that of John Harrington (No. 19). Such executions were so rare in Massachusetts that they had far more impact than in Europe, where the gallows was always full. It was said that on one occasion the ladies present fainted in windrows. The fact that the crime was often rape made the confessions of the criminals the counterparts of the modern tabloid newspapers. Almost as exciting were the accounts of earthquakes (No. 18) and of the revivals carried on by Gilbert Tennent (No. 15) and other emotional preachers. Their crude woodcuts make them the precursors of the modern illustrated news publications.

Graphic and literary art were also combined in the broadside obituary verse (Nos. 2 and 3), a very popular form in an age in which death was ever present. Much more fugitive because less likely to be preserved as having news value were the broadside ballads. Indeed they are so rare that later historians overlooked secular music of the colonial period. They present bibliographical problems because they rarely carry a date or imprint, and cannot easily be distinguished from the English broadside ballads which were imported in great quantities.

Of all of the types of broadsides, the advertisements of merchants and tradesmen have survived in the smallest percentage of those issued. Once read they were made into spills to light pipes because, unlike the Table to Bring Old Tenor into Lawful Money (No. 17), they had no historical interest to suggest that they might be laid away. On the other hand, the merchants of Ulster extraction preserved their Articles Agreed upon by the Charitable Irish Society, in Boston (No. 22). The other large immigrant groups, the indentured servants and the Negroes, had no such organizations, but they are represented in this collection by an advertisement for a runaway servant (No. 23), and by the famous antislavery tract, The Selling of Joseph (No. 10).

In this book are reproduced some of the more interesting examples from the exhibition, which is itself but a sampling from the vast collection in the Massachusetts Historical Society. Like sudden glimpses from the windows of a rapidly traveling train, these broadsides illuminate our past.

CLIFFORD K. SHIPTON

ILLVSTRISSIMIS PIETATE, ET VERA

RELIGIONE, VIRTVTE, ET PRVDENTIA HONORATISSIMIS VIRIS, D. IOHANNI
Winthropo, cæterisque unirarum Nov- Angliæ Coloniarum Gubernatoribus, & Magistratibus Dignissimis;
Vna cum pientissimis, vigilantissimisque Ecclesiarum Presbyteris :

Nec non omnibus nostræ Reip. literariæ, tam in Veteri quam in Nov- Anglia, Fautoribus
benignissimis:

Has Theses Philologicas & Philosophicas, quas σια Θεῶ, Præside Henrico Dunstero palam in
Collegio Harvardino pro virili propugnare conabuntur (honoris, observantiæ et
gratitudinis ergo) D. D. D. in artibus liberalibus initiandi
Adolescentes.

Iohannes Ionesius. Samuel Danforthus.
Samuel Matherus. Iohannes Allinus.

Theses Philologic:

Grammatic.

Linguæ prius discendæ, quam artes.
Linguæ fœlicius usu, quam arte discuntur.
iij Linguarum Anglicana nulli secunda.
iiij Literæ diversæ sonum habent diversum.
v C. et T. efferre ut S. in latinis absurdum.
vi Sheva nec vocalis est, nec consona, nec syllabam e...
Nullæ diphthongi pronunciandæ ut simplices vo...
Syllabarum accentus non destruit tempus.
ix Verba valent sicut nummus.
x Synthesis est naturalis Syntaxis.

Rhetoric:

Rhetorica est affectionum domina.
Eloquentia naturalis excellit artificialem.
iij Apte loqui praestat quam ornate.
iiij Vel gestus fidem facit.

Logic:

Dialectica est omnium artium generalissima.
Efficiens & finis non ingrediuntur rei essentiam.
iij Forma simul cum reipsa ingeneratur.
iv Posita forma ponuntur essentia, differentia & actio.
v Et motus et res motu factæ sunt effecta
vj Oppositorum ex uno affirmato alterum negatur.
vij Relata sunt sibi mutuo causae.
viij Contradictio topica negat ubique.
ix Privantia maxime dissentiunt.
x Genus et species sunt notae causarum et effectorum.
xi Omnis syllogismus est necessarius ratione formae.
xii Omnis quaestio non est subjectum syllogismi.
xiij Methodus procedit ab universalibus ad singularia.

Theses Philosophic:

Ethic:

Fœlicitas moralis est finis Ethices.
... unum actum non generatur h...
iij ...bitus non pereunt sola actuum ce...
i ...s perfecta dari potest, vitium n...
v ...ansa est liberum arbitrium
...ratus in individuo ...
...amentu...
vij Vulgi mos non regeret nos.
ix Est abstinens qui continens.
x Honor sequentem fugit, fugientem sequitur.
xi Diviriæ nil conferunt scelicitati morali.
xij Nulla est vera amicitia inter improbos.

Physic:

Nihil agit in seipsum.
Omnis motus fit in tempore.
iij Non datur infinitum actu.
iiij Pura elementa, non sunt alimenta.
v Non datur proportio arithmetica in mixtis.
vi In uno corpore non sunt plures animae.
vii Anima est tota in toto, & tota in qualibet parte.
viij Status animae in corpore est naturalissimus.
ix Visio fit receptione specierum.
x Phantasia producit reales effectus.
xi Primum cognitum est singulare materiale.

Metaphysic:

Ens qua ens, est objectum metaphysices.
Ente nihil prius, simplicius, melius, verius.
iij Datur discrimen inter ens et rem.
iv Essentia entis non suscipit magis et minus.
v Veritas est conformitas intellectus cum re.

Cantabrigiæ Nov. Ang. Mens. ...
43

No. 1

A
FUNERAL ELEGIE
(Written many years since)
On the Death of the Memorable and truly Honourable

John Winthrope Esq:
Governour *of the* Massachusets Colony in *N-England.*

For the space of 19 years, who died in the 63 d. Year of his Age. *March* 26. 1649

YOu English *Mattachusians* all
  Forbear sometime from sleeping,
Let every one both great and small
  Prepare themselves for weeping.
For he is gone that was our freind,
This Tyrant Death hath wrought his end.
Who was the very Chief among
  The chiefest of our Peers
Who hath in peace maintain'd us long
  The space of nineteen years,
And now hee's breathless, lifeless, dead,
Cold earth is now become his bed.
The Jews did for their *Moses* weep
  Who was their Gubernator,
Let us for *Winthrope* do the like,
  Who was our Conservator
With Lines of gold in Marble stone
  With pens of steel engrave his name
O let the Muses every one
  In prose and Verse extol his Fame,
Exceeding far those ancient Sages
That ruled *Greeks* in former Ages.
O spightfull Death and also cruel
Thou hast quite slain *New-Englands* Jewel :
Shew us vile *Tyrant* if thou can
Tel where to find out such a man ?
Methinks I hear a spirit breathe
Non est inventus here beneath.
He was (we surely may say this)
Rara avis in terris,
Therefore let us give him his due,
  To him is due this stile,
He was an *Israelite* full true
  Without all fraud or guile.
Let *Winthrops* name still famous be,
  With us and our Posterity.
What goods he had he did not spare,
  The Church and Commonwealth
Had of his Goods the greatest share,
  Kept nothing for himself.
My tongue, my pen, my rustick art
Cannot express his true desert.
The nature of the Pelican
Read storyes what they say,
To her I would compare this man
If lawfully I may.
To *Moses* meek, to *Abraham,*
To *Joseph* and to *Jonathan*.
He was *New-Englands* Pelican
New-Englands Gubernator

He was *New-Englands Solomon*
New-Englands Conservator.
Time and Experience the best tryal,
These two admit of no denial:
Let nineteen yeares then witness be
Of *Wintrops* true sincerity.
Such gifts of grace from God had he,
That more than man he seem'd to be.
But now hee's gone and clad in clay,
Grim Death hath taken him away.
Death like a murth'ring Jesuite
Hath rob'd us of our hearts delight.
Let's shew our love to him by weeping
That car'd for us when we lay sleeping.
O that our dry eyes fountains were,
  Our heads a living spring,
O that our sighs the clouds could tear,
  And make an eccho ring:
Let us sit down in sorrow fel,
And now with tears ring out his knel.
Bright shining *Phœbus* hide thy face
Let misty clouds make dark thy sky,
Fair *Cynthia* count it no disgrace
  To aid us with thy weeping eye.
O weep with us for *Joshua*
The Loadstone of *America*.
My sences they are all too weak
His praises due to write or speak
Now I must leave it to their skill
Who can endite and write at well.
New-England thou hast cause to mourn,
For that thy special friend is gone,
Yet see you mourn with moderation,
No cause you have of Desparation,
They yet survive who may renew
Decay'd and dying hopes in you
With honour due let us respect them,
No cause we have for to reject them,
They are to us as true Directors
And under God our chief Protectors.

Here you have *Lowells* loyalty,
  Pen'd with his slender skill
And with it no good poetry,
  Yet certainly good will.
Read these few verses willingly,
And view them not with *Momus* eye,
Friendly correct what is amiss,
Accept his love that did write this.

        Perciful Lowle.

1665

THE
CONDITIONS FOR NEW-PLANTERS
In the Territories of His ROYAL HIGHNES
THE
DUKE OF YORK

THE Purchases are to be made from the *Indian Sachims* and to be Recorded before the *Governour.*

The Purchasers are not to pay for their liberty of purchasing to the *Governour.*

The Purchasers are to set out a Town, and Inhabit together.

No Purchaser shall at any time contract for himself with any *Sachim,* without consent of his Associates: or special Warrant from the *Governour.*

The Purchasers are free from all manner of Assessments or Rates for five years after their Town-plot is set out, and when the five years are expired, they shall only be liable to the publick Rates, and Payments according to the Custome of other Inhabitants both *English* and *Dutch.*

All Lands thus Purchased, and possest shall remain to the Purchasers, and their Heires, as free Lands to dispose of as they please.

In all Territories of his ROYAL HIGHNES, Liberty of Conscience is allowed, Provided such Liberty is not converted to Licentiousness, or the disturbance of others, in the exercise of the Protestant Religion.

The several Townships have liberty to make their peculiar Laws, and Deciding all small Causes within themselves.

The Lands which I intend shall be first Planted, are those upon the West side of *Hudson-River,* at, or adjoyning to the *Sopes,* but if any number of men sufficient for two or three, or more Towns, shall desire to plant upon any other Lands they shall have all due encouragement proportionable to their Quality, and undertakings.

Every Township is Obliged to pay their *Minister,* according to such agreement as they shall make with him, and no man to refuse his Proportion, the *Minister* being elected by the Major part of the Householders Inhabitants of the *Town.*

Every Township hath the free choice of all their officers both Civil, and Military, and all men who shall take the Oath of Allegiance to his *Majesty,* and are not Servants, or day-labourers: but are admitted to enjoy *Town-lotts* are esteemed freemen of the Jurisdiction, and cannot forfeit the same without due process in Law.

R. Nicolls.

Bdar.
Wrentham

At a General Court

Held at Boston *the* 11th *of* Octob.
1675.

WHereas it hath pleased our gracious God, contrary to the many evill-deservings of an unworthy and sinfull People such as we are, so far to espouse the interest of his poor people, as to plead their Cause with the Heathen in this Wilderness, that have risen up against us, and broken in upon many of our Towns and places as a flood, seeking the utter extirpation and ruine of the interest of our Lord Jesus, in this Wilderness, and that with so considerable a progress, and such strange success, as ought not soon to be forgotten by us : in this day of our calamity, God hath made bare his own Arm for our Deliverance, by taking away courage and Counsel from our enemyes, and giving strange advantages and great success to our selves and Confederates against them, that of those several Tribes and Partyes that have risen up against us, which were not a few, there now scarce remains a Name or Family of them in their former habitations, but are either slain, captivated or fled into remote parts of this wilderness, or lye hid despairing of their first intentions against us, at least in these parts : unto which mercy, God hath added an abatement of those Epidemical Sicknesses that have attended us most part of this Summer, and vouchsafed us a liberal portion of the fruits of the earth, for our comfortable sustentation and Relief : The joynt consideration of these things ministers great cause, and the same God that is Author of them, can give us hearts to offer our Praises that thereby we may glorifie him. Which that we may obtain,

THis Court doth appoint and set apart the ninth day of *November* next to be a Day of solemn *Thanksgiving and Praise* to God for such his singular and Fatherly Mercyes bestowed on us : and doe commend the same to the respective Elders, Ministers and People of this Jurisdiction, solemnly and seriously to keep the same.

By the COURT, *Edward Rawson* Secr.

month : day 8th.

1676

At A
COUNCIL,
Held at Charlestown, June the 20th, 1676.

The holy God having by a long and Continued Series of his Afflictive dispensations in & by the present Warr with the Heathen Natives of this Land, written and brought to pass bitter things against his own Covenant people in this wildernefs, yet so that we evidently discern that in the midst of his judgements he hath remembred mercy, having remembred his Foot-stool in the day of his fore displeasure against us for our fins, with many fingular Intimations of his Fatherly Compaffion, and regard: reserving many of our Towns from Desolation Threatned, and attempted by the Enemy, and giving us especially of late with our Confederates many fignal Advantages against them, without such Difadvantage to our felves as formerly we have been fensible of, if it be of the Lords mercies that we are not confumed, It certainly befpeaks our positive Thankfulnefs, when our Enemies are in any meafure disappointed or destroyed: and fearing the Lord should take notice under fo many Intimations of his returning mercy, we should be found an Infenfible people, as not standing before him with Thanksgiving, as well as lading him with our Complaints in the time of preffing Afflictions:

The COUNCIL have thought meet to appoint and set apart the 29th. day of this Instant June, as a day of Solemn Thanksgiving and praise to God for such his goodnefs and Favour, many Particulars of which mercy might be Inftanced, but we doubt not those who are fenfible of Gods Afflictions, have been as diligent to efpy him returning to us; and that the Lord may behold us as a People offering praise and thereby glorifying him; The Council doth Commend it to the Respective Ministers, Elders and people of this Jurisdiction; Solemnly and serioufly to keep the same. Befeeching that being perfwaded by the mercies of God we may all, even this whole people offer up our Bodies and Souls as a living and Acceptable Service unto God by Jefus Christ.

By the Council, Edward Rawson Secr.

A
PROCLAMATION

By The PRESIDENT and COUNCIL of His Majestiy's Territory & Dominion of NEW-ENGLAND in AMERICA.

WHEREAS His Most Excellent Majesty our Soveraign LORD JAMES the Second, King of England, Scotland, France and Ireland, Defender of the Faith &c. by COMMISSION or Letters Patents under His Great Seal of England, bearing Date the Eight day of October in the first year of His Reign hath been graciously pleased to erect and constitute a PRESIDENT and COUNCIL to take Care of all that His Territory and Dominion of New-England called the Massachusetts Bay, the Provinces of New-Hampshire & Main, and the Narraganset Countrey, otherwise called the Kings-Province, with all the Islands, Rights and Members thereunto appertaining; and to Order Rule and GOVERN the same according to the Rules, Methods and Regulations specified in the said Commission: Together with His Majesties Gracious Indulgence in matters of Religion.

And for the Execution of His Royal pleasure in that behalf, His Majesty hath been pleased to appoint Joseph Dudley Esq: to be the first PRESIDENT of His Majesties said Council, & VICE-ADMIRAL of these Seas. And to Continue in the said Offices until his Majesty shall otherwise direct, & also to nominate & appoint William Stoughton, Esq: now Deputy-President, Simon Bradstreet, Robert Mason, John Fitz-Winthrope, John Pynchon, Peter Bulkley, Edward Randolph, Wait Winthrope, Richard Wharton, John Usher, Nathaniel Saltonstal, Bartholomew Gidney, Jonathan Tyng, Dudley Bradstreet, John Hinks, and Edward Tyng, Esq's: to be His Majesties Council in the said Colony and Territories.

The President & Council therefore being convened and having according to the Direction & Form of the said Commission, taken their Oathes and Entered the GOVERNMENT aforesaid; and finding it needful, that speedy & effectual Care be taken for the Observation of His Majesties Commands, and particularly for the Regulation and good Government of the Narraganset Countrey or Kings-Province, which hath hitherto been unsettled. They the said President & Council have resolved speedily to erect and settle a constant Court of Record upon the place; and that the President, Deputy-President, or some others of the Members of His Majesties Council shall be present to give all necessary Power and Directions for Establishing His Majesties Government there, and Administration of Justice to All His Majesties Subjects within the said Narraganset Countrey or Kings-Province, and all the Islands, Rights, and Members thereof. And the said President & Council have in the interim assigned Richard Smith Esq: James Pendleton, and John Foxes Gentlemen, Justices, to keep the Peace of our Soveraign Lord the KING and all His Subjects: And also given Commission to the said Richard Smith to be Sergeant Major, and Chief Commander of His Majesties Militia, both of Horse & Foot within the Narraganset Countrey or Province, and all the Islands Rights and Members thereof. THEREFORE the said President & Council doe hereby, in His Majesties Name and by virtue of His said Commission, strictly Require & Command all other persons being or coming upon the place, to forbear the Exercise of all manner of Jurisdiction, Authority, and Power, and to cease all further Proceedings for the Allotments or Divisions of Land, or making any Strip or Waste upon any part of the said Province, save only on each man's stated Propriety, except by Licence obtained from the said Court, or the President & Council, until there shall be such effectual Regulation and Government established as is directed by His Majesty. And the said President & Council doe hereby henceforth discharge all His Majesties Subjects within the said Narraganset Countrey or Kings Province and all the Islands, Rights & Members thereof from the Government of the Governour & Company of Connecticut & Rhode-Island and Providence Plantation, & all others pretending any Power or Jurisdiction. Hereby Charging & Commanding all His Majesties Subjects to yeild ready & due Obedience to the said Justices of the Peace, the Sergeant Major or Cheif Commander of His Majesties Militia. And George Weightman, Thomas Eldridge, Thomas Monford and William Chaplin are hereby appointed & authorized present Constables: and Liberty given to the aforesaid Justices to appoint so many more as they shall see needful to them, and to administer Oathes unto the aforesaid Constables & such as are to be Ordeined. And all other persons are to be aiding & assisting unto them the said Justices and Constables in the Execution and Discharge of their respective Offices, Charges and Trusts, as they will answer the contrary at their utmost Peril.

Given from the Council-house in Boston this 28th Day of May Anno Domini 1686. Annoq: Regni Regis Jacobi Secundi secundo.

By the President and Council,   Edward Randolph Secr':

GOD SAVE THE KING

BOSTON, in N.E. Printed by Richard Pierce, Printer to the Honourable His Majesties President and Council of this Government.

New England. Proc.

BY HIS EXCELLENCY
A
PROCLAMATION.

Whereas His MAJESTY hath been gracioufly pleafed, by His Royal Letter, bearing Date the fixteenth day of October laft paft, to fignifie That He hath received undoubted Advice that a great and fudden Invafion from *Holland*, with an armed Force of Forreigners and Strangers, will fpeedily be made in an hoftile manner upon His Majefty's Kingdom of *ENGLAND*; and that altho' fome *falfe* pretences relating to *Liberty, Property,* and *Religion,* (contrived or worded with Art and Subtilty) may be given out, (as fhall be thought ufeful upon fuch an Attempt ;) It is manifeft however, (confidering the great Preparations that are making) That no lefs matter by this *Invafion* is propofed and purpofed, than an abfolute Conqueft of His Majefty's Kingdoms, and the utter Subduing and Subjecting His Majefty and all His People to a Forreign Power, which is promoted (as His Majefty underftands) altho' it may feem almoft incredible) by fome of His Majefty's *Subjects,* being perfons of wicked and reftlefs Spirits, implacable Malice, and defperate Defigns, who having no fence of former inteftine Diftractions, (the Memory and Mifery whereof fhould endear and put a Value upon that Peace and Happinefs which hath long been enjoyed) nor being moved by His Majefty's reiterated Acts of Grace and Mercy, (wherein His Majefty hath ftudied and delighted to abound towards all His Subjects, and even towards *thofe* who were once His Majefty's avowed and open *Enemies*) do again endeavour to embroil His Majefty's Kingdom in Blood and Ruin, to gratifie their own Ambition and Malice, propofing to themfelves a Prey and Booty in fuch a publick Confufion :

And that although His Majefty had Notice that a forreign Force was preparing againft Him, yet His Majefty hath alwaies declined any forreign Succour, but rather hath chofen (next under G O D) to rely upon the true and ancient Courage, Faith and Allegiance of His own People, with whom His Majefty hath often ventured His Life for the Honour of His Nation, and in whofe Defence againft all Enemies His Majefty is firmly refolved to live and dye ; and therefore does folemnly *Conjure* His Subjects to lay afide all manner of Animofities, Jealoufies, & Prejudices, and heartily & chearfully to *Unite together* in the Defence of His *MAJESTY* and their native Countrey, which thing alone, will (under GOD) defeat and fruftrate the principal Hope and Defign of His Majefty's Enemies, who expect to find His People divided ; and by publifhing (perhaps) fome plaufible Reafons of their Coming, as the fpecious (tho' *falfe*) Pretences of Maintaining the Proteftant Religion, or Afferting the Liberties and Properties of His Majefty's People, do hope thereby to conquer that great and renowned Kingdom.

That albeit the Defign hath been carried on with all imaginable Secrefie & Endeavours to furprife and deceive His *MAJESTY,* HE hath not been wanting on His part to make fuch provifion as did become Him, and, by GOD's great Bleffing, His Majefty makes no doubt of being found in fo good a Pofture that His Enemies may have caufe to repent fuch their rafh and *unjuft* Attempt. ALL WHICH, it is His Majefty's pleafure, fhould be made known in the moft publick manner to His loving Subjects within this His Territory and Dominion of *NEW-ENGLAND,* that they may be the better prepared to refift any Attempts that may be made by His Majefties Enemies in thefe parts, and fecured in their trade and Commerce with His Majefty's Kingdom of *England.*

I Do therefore, in purfuance of His *MAJESTY's* Commands, by thefe Prefents *make known* and *Publifh* the fame accordingly : And hereby Charge and Command all Officers Civil & Military, and all other His Majefty's loving Subjects within this His Territory and Dominion aforefaid, to be *Vigilant* and *Careful* in their refpective places and ftations, and that, upon the Approach of any Fleet or Forreign Force, they be in Readinefs, and ufe their utmoft Endeavour to hinder any Landing or Invafion that may be intended to be made within the fame.

Given at *Fort-Charles* at *Pemaquid,* the Tenth Day of *January,* in the Fourth year of the Reign of our Sovereign Lord *JAMES* the Second, of *England, Scotland, France* and *Ireland* KING, Defender of the Faith &c. Annoq; DOMINI 1688.

By His EXCELLENCY's Command.
 JOHN WEST. d'. Secr'.

E. ANDROS:

GOD *SAVE THE KING.*

Printed at *Bofton* in *New-England* by R. P.

No. 7

William III
Bolse
c

The PLAIN CASE STATED
Of Old-- but *especially* of *New-England,* in an *Address* to His HIGHNESS

THE PRINCE OF ORANGE·

HAil noble Prince, in whom our Joy and Love
Unite, and (as to their own Center) move.
In whom those Royal Qualities combine
Which may erect a Second *Constantine.*
Among the Songs which *Britain's* joyful dayes
To You present, accept *New-England's* Praise:
VVe also boast our selves of *English* Race :
And from our Ancestors, who stock't this place,
The name of stricter *Protestants* derive,
And in Your faith and favour hope to live.

We heard, (and it to us did Sorrow bring)
The much-lamented death of the late King ;
And, with but too much Truth, did calculate
From thence of all our woes, the wretched Date
Then *James,* with Papal Benediction
And *Popish* principles assum'd the Throne:
A Prince whom Nobler Vertues ne're did yeild
Fitter, the Sceptre of the World to wield :
But to what *Ills* can *Popery* perswade !
And to what *Ruin* do its Maxims lead !
And what a *Hackney* is a *Bigot* made !
Under his umbrage did the Birds of Night
Sing their *damn'd notes,* and sang them with delight;
And Locusts of the Pit, grac't with his Smile,
In swarms invaded our (once happy) Isle.

Heroick *El'sabeth* for us, in vain,
Bafled the fraud of *Rome* and pride of *Spain.*
Whilst Jesuited *James* did readvance
The twisted policies of *Rome* and *France.*

A *Nuncio* from the old Rogue of *Rome*
Must with Applause to *England's* Palace come,
A *Nuncio,* which a Century or more
Of reform'd *England* never saw before;
And we, in grateful sort, must send again
On humble *Embassy* good *Castlemain,*
And, by a *Proxy* kiss his Worship's *Toe,*
Whence *unknown* streames of *unknown* Blessings flow.

From *Innocent* our plotted Ruin came,
Guilty in Fact, tho *Innocent* in Name.
From *France's* Don, whose *Papal-Romish* trade
Of Blood and Ruin has such havock made,
That his *one* Persecution has done more
Than the *ten* under pagan-*Rome* before.
From *Jesuits* a brood, hatch't by the Devil,
To be the Propagators of all evil,
Incarnate Fiends, to Lucifer ally'd,
And heirs to all his cruelty and pride :
From *these,* our *James,* devoted to the Cause
His Measures took, their Counsels were his Laws :

Our *Sanguinary Laws,* tho' few yet good,
And justly merited by men of Blood,
And those with milder penalties inforc't.
Were with a *Prorogation* indors't.
Those Laws, which Parliaments had made to live,
Were laid in dust by Grand Prerogative ;
And *Tests* were useless grown, *Dispensing Power*
Disarm'd their Force, that they could strike no more.
Popery bare-fac't stalk't our injur'd streets,
Justled the Reformation where it meets,
And Cells of *Mass* under our noses grew,
And daring Priests did eagerly pursue
Their Patron's Orders with unbounded joy,
Or to deceive us *Her'ticks,* or destroy.
Dissenting Protestants they strove to please
And wheadle, by a short *delusive* ease.
Th' *establish't* Church trampled, against all Law,
And, *Jehu*--like, drove where they could not draw.
Whilst Renegado-*Papists* were preferr'd,
And had their King's peculiar Regard.
The Snare was laid, the pointed hour drew nigh,
Wherein our *Name* and *Cause* was doom'd to die.
Great were his hopes (who, when the Stroak was gi-
Claim'd for *Reward* a double share of Heaven) [ven
To sacrifice in one brave funeral Pile,
The numerous HERETICKS of either Isle.
Nor could the Vastness of this damn'd design
The Limits of his Popish Rage confine,
But or'e the Ocean to *this* world it flew ;
Reform'd *America* must suffer too.
That *we* were must'red in this bloody Roll
Our *Suffrings* tell (who then could us cajole?)

We, by *Papistick* wiles, may well believe
Were mark't a lingring Ruin to receive.
They grug'd that we should harmlesly possess
With Ease and Freedom this our Wilderness.
Which our religious Ancestors (who sought
God in a Desart Countrey) dearly bought.
Our Charter, which freely we had injoy'd ;
In three successive Reigns, is first made void ;
Condemn'd for forged Crimes we never knew.
Nor at this distance could er'e answer to.
Condemn'd unheard ; their fraud would not admit
A clear Defence and Legal ; nor was't fit
In a Court where *Astraa* nere' did sit.
And thence were we annex't t' a Popish Crown,
By which we were design'd to be undone.

Then came a man to be our President,
As well against the *Law* as our Content :
But he, Alas, did only smooth the way
For a Superior Lord, who made no stay.
Soon came the *Jersy* Knight, crafty and Stout,
And for his Master's Interest cut out.
Soon did he and his Creatures let us know
Whence all our miseries were like to grow.
Knaves, Beggars, *Papists* form'd the triple League
Which carry'd on the ruinous Intreague.
We were not treated by th' insulting Knaves
As free-born *English,* but as poor *French* Slaves.
Taxes were rais'd, without Mercy, or Measure,
To keep us low, and fill our *Tyrant's* Treasure.
To MAGNA CHARTA we coul'd claim no Right,
Neither our own, nor *English* Laws would fit,
But such as by Distortion, and Abuse,
Would still advance the Plot to ruin us.
New Laws by a small shabby Juncto fram'd,
And then so surreptitiously proclaim'd,
As if they chose (Oh when were Laws so made !)
They rather should be broken than obey'd :
So, if we *kept* or *broke* them, 'twas by chance ;
They made advantage of our *Ignorance :*
Strain'd their own Laws beyond their true Intent,
To our great Cost, Sorrow and wonderment.

All that we counted dear was made a Prize
To th' raging Lust and hungry Avarice
Of a few tatter'd Rascals from *New-York,*
More insolent than ever was *Grand Turk.*
Their debanch't tricks the harmless Countrey saw,
But vainly sought a just redress by Law.
The Law, which ev'n our smallest Trips could find
Distinguish't Friends, and in *their* Cause was blind.
Their Lust on Honour strange Excursions made :
Their Avarice did our Estates invade.
Our Lands, for which we to the Natives gave
Their *own Demands* these new-come Beggars crave,
Our Lands, which we had peaceably possess't
For Sixty years, they with strange flaws molest.
It would disturb our Father's peaceful Graves,
Saw they their poor Posterity made slaves,
Or knew our Lives or Liberties betray'd,
Or knew our Lands to forreign Foes convey'd.
Yet thus with grief might poor *New-England* cry,
We *our own Lands* with *our own Coyn* must buy ;
And *Patents* take, or else some sordid Knave
Soon intercepts, and *needs* but *ask and have.*
The Secretaries *House of Office* told
(And Courts of Justice) where our Rights were sold,
New Tricks they found, and Fetches with rare skill,
To bring more Grist to their insatiate Mill.
Money we paid, for what we could not know,
Except to Feed their ever-craving maw,
But never full, for fill we might, as well,
As soon the gaping mouthes of *Death & Hell.*
Law at a price, and Justice we must buy,
Each small Court-Officer gapes for his Fee,
Else Law would be deny'd, and Right delay'd,
Whatever Madam *MAGNA CHARTA* said,
Our *Penal Acts* their *scores & hundreds* slew,
Through cursed aid of an informing Crew.
These in our hated Courts did boldly tread,
Villains, who daily damn'd themselves for bread :
Rogues, who for mony (I in plainness think)
Would swear the *Sun* a bottle full of Ink.

These, Juries must implicitly believe,
And by *their* Testimonies Verdicts give,
The Sense of *Thinking-men* they must forego,
And, as the Court directs them, blindly do,
Else they're turn'd back, and for their honest Strife
Must forfeit the Conveniences of Life.
Juries were pack't out of their own vile lump
To *serve a Turn,* and *turn* them up a *Trump,*
Men of small Sense, and smaller Honesty,
Their knotty roguish Causes to untye.
From Freedom of *Discourse* our Tongues were mor'd,
For we were made Offenders for a word.
When, Mighty Prince, we of Your *Landing* heard,
Tho Hopes & Wishes were on Tip-toes rear'd
Yet *we* our Hopes could *whisp'ring* only tell ;
And bold was he who dar'd to wish You well :
Him shall I style true *Ben,* who hither came,
To save his Life & an untainted fame ;
Harris was he, whom Parliaments had known
T' have been by Popish rage & frauds undone,
Yet *here* he could not scape the Lion's Paw,
Only for wishing well to *WILLIAM o' Nassau.*
Our *last* great Grievance, which we could not bear
(With *Grief* we *tell,* and Oh, with *Pity hear !*)
Was a perplex't mysterious *Indian-War,*
For which with mighty Forces we prepare.
We, who a *Hundred,* in the days of yore
Could beat a *Thousand Indians* and fight *more,*
An Army now a thousand strong must send,
With a poor Handful Hundred to contend ;
In horrid Woods where no Provision grew,
Sneaking moneths after moneths to ly *perdue.*
Our Officers were Popish men of blood,
Whose Principles could nere consult our Good.
Our Scatt'ring Foes but seldom came in sight,
Or if they had, we had no power to fight ;
No War was ere *proclaim'd ;* what could we do?
We dare not kill, the *Law* would then pursue.
Mean time a tedious *Winter* past our head,
Our Suffrings such, we envy'd ev'n our *dead.*
And they not few by sore Diseases went.
Hunger and *Cold,* and how could this content ?
And thus things stood, and thus the Plot went on,
From earth to root our Her'tick Nation
Here, and in our beloved Native Isle ;
Till Heaven on us cast a propitious smile,
Piti'd our wrongs and on their Counsels frown'd,
And rais'd a man their Empire to confound.
'Twas YOU, Great Sir, whom Heav'n did elevate
To make more famous this our *Eighty Eight*
Than that wherein brave *El'sabeth* did quell
The jointed pow'rs of *Spain & Rome & Hell.*
YOU, us with gallant Forces did Invade,
(By long Successes formidable made)
Our wishes join'd and met our hearts half way,
Whilst Terror seiz'd our popish foes that day.
One bloodless month our happy Nation freed
From popish Plots, by which we fear'd to bleed;
Founded a crew of mercenary Knaves.
Jesuits & Priests, tools us'd to make us Slaves.
Frighted our stubborn King, who would not part
From his dear *Bantling,* nor his *Bigot-heart.*
Conven'd our Countrey's Representative,
By whose sage Counsels we now hope to live.

This hearing, by Your great Example sway'd,
A *just* Attempt opprest *New-England* made,
Not to revenge our wrongs but set us free
From *arbitrary Power* and *Slavery :*
This did Heav'n bless, and on our Action smile,
Befool'd our foes, and brought them to the Toyl.
Sir, Your Protection we hope and crave ;
Condemn not the Success Your Courage gave.
For this our Songs shall Your brave Triumphs meet,
Laying our Lives and fortunes at Your Feet :
For *this* Your Name will consecrated be
In *English* Hearts to late Posterity.
May still Success Your great Atchievements crown!
Go on to *Conquer,* as You have begun.

BOSTON, Printed for and Sold by
Benjamin Harris at the London Coffee-house.

No. 8

A RELATION
OF
Captain Bull,
Concerning the
MOHAVVKS
At FORT-ALBANY. May, 1689.

Connecticot *Colony upon many Rumours of Hazzard, sent Captain* Jonathan Bull *to* Albany *to inform the* Albanians *of the News from* England *we had Received; and what Change was made in the Bay, who seemed much Rejoyced ; Declaring they'd allow the Fort to Remain not twelve Hours longer in* Papists Hands : *That being noised about, Major* Baxter *Declared he'd Remove in four or five Days, which accordingly he did, leaving the Fort to the Inhabitants, who have placed twenty five* Men *in it for the best.*

The *English* and *Dutch* there are very sure of the Friendliness of the *Mohawks,* and the five other Nations above them.

May 24. The *Mohawk Sachems,* appeared in the Court-House of *Albany,* with a Present of Beaver of about twenty pound value, who chose their Speaker, he taking two or three Skins, the rest sitting silent, Rose up and said :

1. Brethren, we are now come as our Grandfathers used to do, to Renew our Unity, Friendship and Covenant made by us and you.

2 We desire the House, being the Covenant and Proposition House may be kept clean, that we may keep a clean, single, and not a double heart.

3. We do now Renew the Former Covenant or Claim that hath been made between us and you ; (*viz.*) *New-England, Virginia, Mary-land,* and those parts of *America,* that it may be kept bright on every side, and not suffered to rust, or be forgotter.

4. We are heartily sorry to hear of the Bloodshed by those ill minded *Indians* to the *Eastward*; and we now Present this Guift as our *Indian* manner is, to wipe the Tears from the Eyes, and the Blood from off the Relations of those who have lost Friends by those ill-minded men.

5. Let the Tree of Love, Unity and Commerce grow and flourish, and let the Roots spread and branch forth through all our several Dominions, to stand fast that none may move it; so that we may live under the shade of the Tree, so that the Sun of Discord and Quarrelling may not scorch and wound us.

6. We have heard there hath been several Embassyes the last year from you to *Canady,* that we could not be acquainted with, we do all publickly Above-board, and we desire you do so also.

We heard that the *Eastern Indians* came where some of our men were Hunting, desirous to speak with us, but we refused to have any discourse with them, but warned them to be gone, so that they came not near our Forts, but went as they came.

7. We intend a Meeting of the Chief of our five Nations in a little time, at *Amadado,* there further to consider of publick Affairs, and desire that you would send some persons from you to hear what we shall Confer of, and also some of the *River Indians* if they see cause, the Meeting was chiefly intended to consider what Answer to give the *French,* who had often sent to have Speech with them.

VVhen the *Sachems* had heard how Matters were circumstanced, in the Country, and what News was come to hand, seemed to be glad, and much Rejoiced, & wholly laid aside their intended Meeting, promising neither to speak with them, nor to allow the *French* to speak to them.

The *Dutch* at *Albany* say, the *Mohawks* shew themselves very willing to go against the *Eastern Indians,* if Desired.

Mass. Hist. Society from Rob. C. Winthrop.
Oct. 8. 1863.

The Selling
OF
JOSEPH
A Memorial.

FORASMUCH *as Liberty is in real value next unto Life: None ought to part with it themselves, or deprive others of it, but upon most mature Consideration.*

The Numerousness of Slaves at this day in the Province, and the Uneasiness of them under their Slavery, hath put many upon thinking whether the Foundation of it be firmly and well laid; so as to sustain the Vast Weight that is built upon it. It is most certain that all Men, as they are the Sons of *Adam*, are Coheirs; and have equal Right unto Liberty, and all other outward Comforts of Life. G O D *hath given the Earth [with all its Commodities] unto the Sons of Adam, Psal 115. 16. And hath made of One Blood, all Nations of Men, for to dwell on all the face of the Earth, and hath determined the Times before appointed, and the bounds of their habitation: That they should seek the Lord.* Forasmuch then as we are the Offspring of G O D &c. *Act 17.26,27,29.* Now although the Title given by the last ADAM, doth infinitely better Mens Estates, respecting GOD and themselves; and grants them a most beneficial and inviolable Lease under the Broad Seal of Heaven, who were before only Tenants at Will: Yet through the Indulgence of GOD to our First Parents after the Fall, the outward Estate of all and every of their Children, remains the same, as to one another. So that Originally, and Naturally, there is no such thing as Slavery. *Joseph* was rightfully no more a Slave to his Brethren, than they were to him: and they had no more Authority to *Sell* him, than they had to *Slay* him. And if *they* had nothing to do to Sell him; the *Ishmaelites* bargaining with them, and paying down Twenty pieces of Silver, could not make a Title. Neither could *Potiphar* have any better Interest in him than the *Ishmaelites* had. *Gen. 37. 20, 27, 28.* For he that shall in this case plead *Alteration of Property*, seems to have forfeited a great part of his own claim to Humanity. There is no proportion between Twenty Pieces of Silver, and LIBERTY. The Commodity it self is the Claimer. If *Arabian* Gold be imported in any quantities, most are afraid to meddle with it, though they might have it at easy rates; lest it it should have been wrongfully taken from the Owners, it should kindle a fire to the Consumption of their whole Estate. 'Tis pity there should be more Caution used in buying a Horse, or a little lifeless dust; than there is in purchasing Men and Women: Whenas they are the Offspring of GOD, and their Liberty is,
————— *Auro pretiosior Omni.*

And seeing GOD hath said, *He that Stealeth a Man and Selleth him, or if he be found in his hand, he shall surely be put to Death. Exod. 21. 16.* This Law being of Everlasting Equity, wherein Man Stealing is ranked amongst the most atrocious of Capital Crimes: What louder Cry can there be made of that Celebrated Warning,

Caveat Emptor !

And

By the HONORABLE,
Thomas Povey Esq.
Lieutenant GOVERNOUR, and Commander in Chief, for the time being,
of Her Majesties Province of the *Massachusetts-Bay* in *New-England.*

A Proclamation.

WHEREAS *John Quelch,* late Commander of the Briganteen *Charles,* and Company to her belonging, *Viz.* John Lambert, John Miller, John Clifford, John Dorothy, James Parrot, Charles James, William Whiting, John Pitman, John Templeton, Benjamin Perkins, William Wiles, Richard Lawrance, Erasmus Peterson, John King, Charles King, Isaac Johnson, Nicholas Lawson, Daniel Chevalle, John Way, Thomas Farrington, Matthew Primer, Anthony Holding, William Rayner, John Quittance, John Harwood, William Jones, Denis Carter, Nicholas Richarson, James Austin, James Pattison, Joseph Hutnot, George Peirse, George Norton, Gabriel Davis, John Breck, John Carter, Paul Giddins, Nicholas Dunbar, Richard Thurbar, Daniel Chuley, and others ; Have lately Imported a considerable Quantity of Gold dust, and some Bar and Coin'd Gold, which they are Violently Suspected to have gotten and obtained, by Felony and Piracy, from some of Her Majesties Friends and Allies, and have Imbezel'd and Shared the same among themselves, without any Adjudication or Condemnation thereof, to be lawful Prize. The said Commander and some others being apprehended, and in Custody, the rest are absconded and fled from Justice.

I have therefore thought fit, by and with the Advice of Her Majesties Council, strictly to Command and Require all Officers Civil and Military, and other Her Majesties Loving Subjects, to Apprehend and Seize the said Persons, or any of them, whom they may know or find, and them secure and their Treasure, and bring them before one of the Council, or next Justice of the Peace, in order to their being safely Conveyed to Boston, to be Examined and brought to Answer what shall be Objected against them, on Her Majesties behalf.

And all Her Majesties Subjects, and others, are hereby strictly forbiden to entertain, harbour or conceal any of the said Persons, or their Treasure ; Or to convey away, or in any manner further the Escape of any of them, on pain of being proceeded against with utmost Severity of Law, as accessaries and partakers with them in their Crime.

Given at the Council Chamber in *Boston* the *Twenty-fourth* Day of *May* : In the Third Year of the Reign of our Sovereign Lady *ANNE,* by the Grace of GOD of *England, Scotland, France* and *Ireland,* QUEEN, Defender of the Faith, *&c.* Annoque Domini. 1704.

By Order of the Lieut.
Governour & Council,
Isaac Addington Secr.

T. POVEY.

GOD Save the Queen.

BOSTON: Printed by *Bartholomew Green,* Printer to His Excellency the GOVERNOUR and COUNCIL. 1704.

The Names of the STREETS, Lanes & Alleys,

Within the Town of *Boston* in *New-England.*

At a Meeting of the Free-holders and other Inhabitants of the Town of Boston, *duely Qualified & Warned according to Law, being Convened at the Town-house, the 22d. day of* September, Anno Domini. 1701.

Voted, That the Select-men of this Town are impowered to Assign & Fix Names, unto the several Streets and Lanes within this Town, as they shall judge meet & convenient.

At a Meeting of the Select-men of the Town of Boston, *the 3d. day of* May, Anno Domini, 1708.

Ordered, That the Streets, Lanes and Alleys, of this Town, as they are now (by the said Select-men) Named and Bounded, be accordingly recorded in the Town Book, and are as followeth, *viz.*

1. THE broad Street or Way from the Old Fortification on the Neck, leading into the Town as far as the late Deacon *Eliot's* corner. **Orange Street.**

2. The Way below the late Deacon *Eliot's* Barn, leading from Orange Street Easterly by the Sea Side. **Beech Street.**

3. The Way leading Easterly from the said Deacon *Eliot's* corner, passing by the late Deacon *Allens*, extending to Windmill point. **Essex Street.**

4. The Way leading from the late Elder *Ransfords* corner in Essex Street, extending Southerly into Beech Street, and so down to the Sea. **Ransfords Lane.**

5. The Way leading from the late Capt. *Fraryes* corner Westerly, to the bottom of the Common, with the return Southerly down to the Sea. **Frogg Lane.**

6. The Street from the corner of the House now in the Tenure of Capt. *Turfrey*, nigh Deacon *Eliots* corner, leading Northerly as far as Dr. *Oakes's* corner. **Newbury Street.**

7. The New Alley between Mr. *Blyns* & *Durants* in Newbury Street, leading Westerly into the Common. **Hogg Alley.**

8. The Street leading Easterly from *Wheelers* corner in Newbury Street, passing by the Towns Watering place, as far as Capt. *Dyers* Barn. **Pond Street.**

9. The Way leading from *John Ushers* Esq. his Barn Southerly into Essex Street. **Short Street.**

10. The Way leading from the lower end of Pond-street, North-Easterly into Church Green, by Summer Street. **Blind Lane.**

11. The Way from *Cowels* corner in Newbury Street, leading Westerly into the Common. **West Street.**

12. The Way from *Ellise's* corner nigh the upper end of Summer Street, leading Westerly into the Common. **Winter Street.**

13. The Street leading Easterly from Dr. *Oake's* corner in Newbury Street, passing by the House of Capt. *Timothy Clark*, extending to the Sea. **Summer Street.**

14. The Street from *Baxters* corner in Summer Street, leading Southerly by the late Deacon *Allens*, extending down to the Sea. **South Street.**

15. The Way from *Bulls* corner at the lower end of Summer Street, leading Southerly to Windmill point. **Sea Street.**

16. The Street leading from *Penemans* corner at the upper end of Summer Street, passing by the South Meeting-house, to Mr. *Haugh's* corner. **Malborough Street.**

17. The Way leading from *Briscows* corner in Marlborough Street passing by Justice *Bromfields* into the Common **Rawsons Lane.**

18. The Way leading from the South Meeting-house, passing by Mr. *Borlands*, and so down to the Sea by *Mr. Hallawars.* **Milk Street.**

19. The Alley leading Southerly from *Southers* corner in Milk Street, to Capt. *Clarks* corner in Summer Street. **Bishops Alley.**

20. The Lane leading South-Easterly from Mr. *Borland's* corner in Milk-Street to *Beards* corner in Cow Lane. **Long Lane.**

21. The Street where Mr. *Daniel Oliver* dwells, passing from Milk-Street up to Fort-Hill. **Oliver Street.**

22. The Way leading Southerly from Fort-Hill to *Morey's* corner in Summer Street. **Cow Lane.**

23. The Way from the lower end of Summer Street, leading North-Easterly by the Sea Side, with the return up to the Rope Walk. **Flownder Lane.**

24. The Alley by *Whartons* house in Cow-lane, leading Easterly into *Harrisons* Rope Walk. **Crooked Alley.**

25. The Way from *John Roberts's* house in Cow Lane, leading Easterly by Capt *Bonners*, into the Rope walk. **Gridley's Lane.**

26. The Way from the upper end of Cow Lane on Fort Hill leading Easterly, passing by *Mr. Joseph Hubberts* down to the Sea. **Gibbs's Lane.**

27. The Way leading from the Northerly Side of Fort Hill passing down Easterly by the Old Brew-house into Battery March. **Sconce Lane.**

28. The Way leading from *Hallaway's* corner by the end of Milk Street, passing by the Battery, extending to the lower end of *Gibbs's* Lane. **Battery March.**

29. The Way leading Southerly from *Gibbs's* Lane on Fort Hill, passing by *Drinkers* to the Rope-walk. **Belchers Lane.**

30. The Way from Mr. *Haugh's* corner, leading Northwesterly by the Latin School, extending as far as Mrs. *Whetcombs* corner. **School Street.**

31. The Way leading from Mrs. *Whetcombs* corner westerly through the upper side of the Common, and so down to the Sea. **Beacon Street.**

32. The Way leading from Beacon Street, on the upper side of the Common unto Mr. *Allens* Orchard. **Davies Lane.**

33. The Way leading from Beacon Street, between Capt *Alfords* and Madam *Shrimptons* Pasture, up to Centry Hill **Centry Street.**

34. The Street from the lower end of School Street, leading Northerly as far as Mr. *Clarks* the Pewterers Shop. **Corn-Hill.**

35. The Way leading from a Tenement of Capt. *Clark's* nigh the lower end of School Street, to Mrs. *Winslows* corner in *Joyliffs* lane. **Spring Lane.**

36. The Street leading from *Cox* the Butchers Shop in Cornhill, passing by Major *Walleys*, as far as the corner of *Mr. Olivers Brick Ware-house.* **Water Street.**

37. The Alley leading from the end of Water-Street, through Mr. *Olivers* Land by *Odell's* into Milk Street. **Coopers Alley.**

38. The Way leading from Water Street, passing between Major *Walley's* and Mr. *Bridghams* Lands into Milk Street. **Tanners Lane.**

39. The Lane passing from Water Street into Milk Street, according to the Name by which it hath been formerly known. **Joyliefs Lane.**

40. The Way passing Round the Old Meeting-House. **Church Square.**

41. The Way leading from Corn Hill, including the Wayes on each side of the Town House, extending Easterly to the Sea. **King Street.**

42. The Street leading from Mr. *Derings* corner in Corn Hill to *Houchen's* corner at the upper end of Hanover Street. **Queen Street.**

43. The Way leading from the Mansion House of the late *Simon Lynde* Esq. by Capt. *Southacks*, extending as far as Col. *Townsends* corner. **Trea Mount Street.**

44. The Way leading from *Melyen's* corner near Col. *Townsends*, passing through the Common along by Mr. *Sheafs* into Frog Lane. **Common Street.**

45. The Alley leading Easterly from the Common, on the North side of Madam *Ushers* House. **Turn again Alley.**

46. The Way leading from the Exchange in King Street, passing by Mrs. *Phillips's* into Water Street. **Pudding Lane.**

47. The Way leading from King Street, by the House of *Isaac Addington* Esq. with the Return into Pudding Lane. **Half-square Court.**

48. The Way leading from Mr. *Mackarty's* corner in King Street, to Elder *Bridghams* Ware-House in Water street. **Leverets Lane.**

49. The way leading from Justice *Dummers* corner in King-street, passing over the Bridge as far as Mrs. *Dassons* corner in Milk-street. **Mackeril Lane.**

50. The way leading from the House formerly the Castle-Tavern in Mackeril-lane, passing by Mr. *Hallaways* wharffe to the Sea. **Crabb Lane.**

51. The Way leading from the Sign of the Orange Tree, passing by Mr. *Stephen Minots* to the Mill Pond, and from thence to the lower end of Cold-lane. **Sudbury Street.**

52. The way leading from *Emmons's* corner passing by the Justice *Lynde's* Pasture, extending from thence westerly to the Sea. **Cambridge Street.**

53. The way passing on the Northerly side of Livery-stable, in Justice *Lynds's* Pasture, to Mr. *Allens* Farm-house. **Green Lane.**

54. The way from Mr. *Powning's* corner by Dock-square, leading *Southerly* into King-street. **Crooked Lane.**

55. The square from the House of *Eliakim Hutchinsons* Esq. to Mr. *Pembertons* corner on the one side, and from *Kenny's* Shop to Mr. *Meers's* corner on the other side. **Dock Square.**

56. The way leading from Major *Savage's* corner in Dock-square, to Madam *Shrimptons* corner in King-street. **Shrimptons Lane.**

57. The way leading from Mr *Meers's* corner along by the side of the Dock, as far as the corner of the Ware-House, formerly Major *Davis's*. **Corn Market.**

58. The Alley leading from Mr. *Mountforts* in Corn Market, to Capt. *Fitch's* corner in King-street. **Pierses Alley.**

59. The way leading from *Justice Palmers* Ware-House in Corn-market, up to *Mr. Moorcocks* buildings. **Corn Court.**

60. The way leading from Mrs. *Butlers* corner, at the lower end of King-street, to the Swinging Bridge, & from thence to the lower end of *Woodmansies* Wharffe. **Merchants Row.**

61. The way leading from *Platt's* corner, passing Northwesterly by the Sign of the Dragon to the Mill Pond. **Union Street.**

62. The Street from between *Houchens's* corner and the Sign of the Orange Tree, leading Northerly to the Mill Bridge. **Hanover Street.**

63. The way leading from Mr. *Pembertons* corner at the end of Dock-square, to Justice *Lyde's* corner in Hanover-street. **Wings Lane.**

64. The way leading from *Wings* Lane to Mr. *Colmans* Church, and from thence the two ways, *viz. Southerly* to Queen-street, and *Easterly* to Dock-square. **Brattle Street.**

65. The new way leading from Mr. *Pollords* corner in *Brattle*-street, thro' Mr. *Belknaps* Yard into Queen-street **Hilliers Lane.**

66. The way leading Northwesterly from Mr. *Harris's* corner in Hanover-street, down to the Mill Pond. **Cold Lane.**

67. The way leading from Capt. *Ballantines* corner nigh the Mill-bridge, to the corner of Capt. *Fitches* Tenement in Union Street. **Marshalls Lane.**

68. The way leading from *Brooks's* corner in Marshalls Lane, passing by Mr. *Bulfinches*, to Scottows Alley. **Creek Lane.**

69. The way leading from Creek Lane to Capt. *Lows* corner, in Union Street. **Salt Lane.**

70. The way leading from Creek Lane, to Mr. *Webbs* corner in Union *Street.* **Marsh Lane.**

71. The way leading from the sign of the Star in Hanover Street passing Northerly behind Capt. *Evertons* house **Link Ally.**

72. the way from the Conduit in Union Street, leading Northerly over the Bridge to *Ellistons* corner, at the lower end of Cross Street. **Anne Street.**

73. The way from Mr. *Antrams* corner nigh the Conduit, leading North-easterly by the side of the Dock, as far as Mr. *Winsors* Ware-house. **Fish Market.**

74. The New way from Union Street, passing Southwesterly between the buildings of the late Capt. *Christopher Clark* deceased. **Minots Court.**

75. The Alley by Capt. *Abijah Savages* in Anne Street, leading Northwesterly to Creek Lane. **Scottows Alley.**

76. The way between Capt. *Winsors* and Mrs. *Pembertons*, in Anne Street, leading to the Wharfes by the Swinging Bridge. **Swingbridge Lane.**

77. The Street from Mount-joys corner at the lower end of Cross Street, leading Northerly to the Sign of the Swan by Scarlets Wharfe. **Fish Street.**

78. The Way leading Northwesterly from Mr. *Thomas's* corner in Anne Street. **Paddeys Alley.**

79. The Street leading from the Mill Bridge Northerly, as far as Mr. *Jonas Clarks* corner at the end of *Bennet Street.* **Middle Street.**

80. The way leading Northerly from *Stanburyes* corner nigh the Mill Bridge, as far as Mr. *Gees* corner in Prince-street. **Back Street**

81. The way leading from the Mill Pond *South-Easterly*, by the late Deacon *Phillips's* Stone-house, extending down to the *Sea.* **Cross Street.**

82. The way from the *North-westerly* end of *Cross Street* passing by *Verings* house *Northerly* nigh the Mill Pond. **Old Way.**

83. The Lane leading from *Middle Street*, passing by the House of the late Capt. *Timothy Prout*, into *Fish Street*, and so down to the Sea. **Wood Lane.**

84. The way from *Wales's* corner in *Middle Street*, leading North-westerly into Back-street. **Beer Lane.**

85. The Alley leading from *Anne Street*, between the late Capt. *Lakes* and *Nanneys* buildings, to Mr. *Indecots* shop in Cross-street. **Elbow Alley.**

86. The Alley leading from *Fish Street* between the Lands of *John Clark* Esq. and the successors of Mr. *Samuel Gallop* Deceased, into Middle-street. **Gallops Alley.**

87. The *Street* leading Northwesterly from *Morses* corner in Middle-street, passing by the House formerly the sign of the BlackHorse, extending to the *Sea* at Ferry-way. **Prince Street**

88. The Street leading Northerly from the end of *Bennet Street*, nigh Mr. *Jonas Clarks*, extending to the Sea. **North Street.**

89. The Street leading *South-Easterly* from *Williams's* corner, nigh Mr. *Jonas Clarks* down to the Sea, by *Scarletts Wharffe.* **Fleet Street.**

90. The Alley leading *North-Westerly* from the North Meeting-House into Middle-street. **Bell Alley**

91. The Square lying on the Southerly side of the North-Meeting-House, including the ways on each side of the Watch-House. **Clarks Square.**

92. The Way leading South Easterly from the North-Meeting-House into Fish Street. **Sun Court.**

93. The Way leading from the North-Meeting-House Northerly by Capt. *Tho. Barnards* into Fleet Street. **Moon Street.**

94. The Way leading Northerly from Mrs. *Winsleys* corner between Col. *Foster's* and Mr. *Frizzel's* into Fleet Street. **Garden Court.**

95. The Street leading Northerly from *Mr. Everton's* corner, nigh *Scarlet's Wharffe*, to the North Battery. **Ship Street.**

96. The Way leading North-Westerly from the North-Battery, to the Ferry way by *Hudson's* Point. **Lyn Street.**

97. The Way leading Westerly along the shore from *Hudson's* Point to the Mill Stream by Mr. *Gee's* Ship yard. **Ferry Way.**

98. The Street leading North-Westerly, from Mrs. *Ransford's* Corner in North Street towards the Ferry Point at *Charles Town.* **Charter Street.**

99. The Way leading from *Carwithys* Corner in Prince Street, to Mr. *Phips's* Corner in Charter Street. **Salem Street.**

100. The Way leading Northerly from *Travis's* Corner in Prince Street, to the end of Ferry-way by *Hudsons* Point. **Snow Hill.**

101. The Way leading South Easterly from Snow Hill to Salem Street. **Hull Street.**

102. The Way leading North-westerly from Mr. *Jonas Clarks* Corner to Salem Street. **Bennet Street.**

103. The Way leading N. westerly from Capt. *Stevenes's* Corner in N. Street, with the return into Bennet Street. **Love Street.**

104. The Alley leading from the Burying place in Charter Street to *Adkins's* Lime Kiln in Lyn Street. **Lime Alley.**

105. The Alley leading from Charter-street down by *Benj. Williams's* in Lyn-street. **Sliding Alley.**

106. The Way leading from Charter-street down by Mrs. *Buckley's* into Lyn-street. **Henchmans Lane.**

107. The Alley Leading from Charter-street down through Mr *Greenoughs* Ship Yard into Lyn-street **Greenoughs Alley.**

108. The Alley leading from North-street down by the Salutation into Ship-street. **Salutation Alley.**

109. The Alley leading from North-street along by *Mr. Will. Parkmans* into Ship-street near the North Battery. **Battery Alley.**

110. The Alley leading from North-street down to Capt. *Richards's* corner in Ship-street. **White Bread Alley.**

BOSTON: Printed by *Bartholomew Green*, in Newbury Street: Sold by the Booksellers. 1708. *Price 3d.*

The Grammarians Funeral,

OR,

An ELEGY composed upon the Death of Mr. *John Woodmancy*,
formerly a School-Master in *Boston* : But now Published upon
the DEATH of the Venerable

Mr. Ezekiel Chevers,

The late and famous School-Master of *Boston* in *New-England* ; Who Departed this Life the
Twenty-first of *August* 1 7 0 8. Early in the Morning. In the Ninety-fourth Year of his Age.

EIght Parts of *Speech* this Day wear *Mourning Gowns*
Declin'd *Verbs, Pronouns, Participles, Nouns.*
And not declined, *Adverbs* and *Conjunctions,*
In *Lillies* Porch they stand to do their functions.
With *Preposition* ; but the most affection
Was still observed in the *Interjection.*
The *Substantive* seeming the limbed best,
Would set an hand to bear him to his Rest.
The *Adjective* with very grief did say,
Hold me by strength, or I shall faint away.
The Clouds of Tears did over-cast their faces,
Yea all were in most lamentable *Cases.*
The five *Declensions* did the Work decline,
And *Told* the *Pronoun Tu,* The work is thine :
But in this case those have no call to go
That want the *Vocative,* and can't say O !
The *Pronouns* said that if the *Nouns* were there,
There was no need of them, they might them spare :
But for the sake of *Emphasis* they would,
In their Discretion do what ere they could.
Great honour was confer'd on *Conjugations,*
They were to follow next to the *Relations.*
Amo did love him best, and *Doceo* might
Alledge he was his Glory and Delight.
But *Lego* said by me he got his skill,
And therefore next the *Herse* I follow will.
Audio said little, hearing them so hot,
Yet knew by him much Learning he had got.
O *Verbs* the *Active* were, Or *Passive* sure,
Sum to be *Neuter* could not well endure.
But this was common to them all to Moan
Their load of grief they could not soon *Depone.*
A doleful Day for *Verbs,* they look so *moody,*
They drove Spectators to a Mournful Study.
The *Verbs* irregular, 'twas thought by some,
Would break no rule, if they were pleas'd to come.
Gaudeo could not be found ; fearing disgrace
He had with-drawn, sent *Mæreo* in his Place.
Possum did to the utmost he was able,
And bore as Stout as if he'd been A *Table.*

Volo was willing, *Nolo* some-what stout,
But *Malo* rather chose, not to stand out.
Possum and *Volo* wish'd all might afford
Their help, but had not an *Imperative Word.*
Edo from Service would by no means Swerve,
Rather than fail, he thought the *Cakes* to Serve.
Fio was taken in a fit, and said,
By him a Mournful *P O E M* should be made.
Fero was willing for to bear a part,
Altho' he did it with an aking heart.
Feror excus'd, with grief he was so Torn,
He could not bear, he needed to be born.
Such *Nouns* and *Verbs* as we defective find,
No *Grammar* Rule did their attendance bind.
They were excepted, and exempted hence,
But *Supines,* all did blame for negligence.
Verbs Offspring, *Participles* hand-in-hand,
Follow, and by the same direction stand :
The rest Promiscuously did croud and cumber,
Such Multitudes of each, they wanted Number.
Next to the Corps to make th' attendance even,
Jove, Mercury, Apollo came from heaven.
And *Virgil, Cato,* gods, men, Rivers, Winds,
With *Elegies,* Tears, Sighs, came in their kinds.
Ovid from *Pontus* hast's Apparrell'd thus,
In Exile-weeds bringing *De Tristibus* :
And *Homer* sure had been among the Rout,
But that the Stories say his Eyes were out.
Queens, Cities, Countries, Islands, Come
All Trees, Birds, Fishes, and each Word in *Um.*
What *Syntax* here can you expect to find ?
Where each one bears such discomposed mind.
Figures of Diction and Construction,
Do little : Yet stand sadly looking on.
That such a Train may in their motion *chord,*
Prosodia gives the measure Word for Word.

Sic Mæstus Cecinit,

Benj. Tompson.

Daniel D Bradford
1825
from J. M.

By the HONOURABLE
William Dummer, Esq;

Lieutenant GOVERNOUR and Commander in Chief in and over His Majesties Province of the *Massachusetts-Bay* in *New-England.*

A PROCLAMATION
For Apprehending *Henry Phillips.*

WHEREAS a barbarous Murder was last Night committed on the Body of Mr. **Benjamin Woodbridge**, a Young Gentleman Resident in the Town of **Boston**, and **Henry Phillips** of said Town is Suspected to be the Author of the said Murder, and is now fled from Justice;

I **Have therefore thought fit to Issue this Proclamation, hereby Commanding all Justices, Sheriffs, Constables, and all other Officers within this Province, and Requiring all others in His Majesties Name to use their utmost Endeavours** that the said Henry Phillips **may be apprehended and brought to Justice; And all Persons whatsoever are Commanded at their utmost Peril not to Harbour or Conceal him. The said** Henry Phillips **is a fair Young Man about the Age of Twenty-two Years, well set, and well dress'd, and has a Wound in one of his Hands.**

Given at *Boston* the *Fourth* Day of *July* 1728. In the Second Year of the Reign of our Sovereign Lord *GEORGE* the Second, by the Grace of GOD of *Great Britain, France* and *Ireland*, KING, Defender of the Faith, &c.

By Order of the Honourable
the Lieut. Governour,

Josiah Willard, Secr.

W. DUMMER.

GOD save the KING.

BOSTON: Printed by *B. Green*, Printer to His Honour the Lieut. GOVERNOUR. 1728.

Daniel D Bradford

ON THE
Reverend Mr. *Gilbert Tennent's*

Powerful and succefsful Preaching in *Boston*, and other neigh-
bouring Towns.   With a few Words of Advice to awaken'd
Souls.   And of Warning to the Difpifers of the Gofpel
Offers of Salvation

WE blefs the Man fent by the Spirit of Grace
⠀⠀To turn poor Sinners into Wifdom's Ways ;
⠀⠀To plow the barr'n and break the fallow Ground,
⠀⠀Diffect the Heart and fhew the mortal Wound.
There's few like him that ever we have feen,
Since lovely *Whitefield*-----O ! how fharp and keen.
He weilds GOD's Law----the Holy Spirit's Sword,
And wound the Heart at almoft every Word,
A *Boanerges* fometimes he'l appear,
And then a fweet and lovely Comforter.
So fkilful Surgeons firft rip up the Wound,
Then ply their Medicines 'till the Patient's found,
The fafe Profeffor's by him tri'd and caft,
He fhews the Doom they're fure to have at laft.
The Formalift he fearches to the Root,
And fhews they bring forth nought but rotten Fruit.
The Hypocrite he doth anatomize,
Shews they're made up of fordid Falicies.
When he founds forth the Thunders of the Law,
He ftrikes the Soul with Trembling and with Awe,
And when the Gofpel Charms he doth difplay,
On Wings of Faith believing Souls away.
They mount, they fly unto the bleft Abode
Where JESUS reigns the great incarnate GOD.
While he fets forth the great Redeemer's Charms,
They foar aloft into his bleffed Arms.
While for his Mafter's Son a Spoufe he woos,
With pearly Drops his lovely Cheeks bedews.
What mad befotted Difperado can
Take Prejudice againft this holy Man ?
When all he feeks and with his Soul doth crave,
Is precious and immortal Souls to fave,
While fcoffing *Ifhmaels* rufh into the Fire,
I'll fear GOD's Wrath, I'll tremble at his Ire.
While HELL without a Covering they court,
I to the dear Redeemer will refort.
I'll hear the Call the lovely *Tennent* brings,
Becaufe I know it's from the King of Kings.
When *Jonah* unto *Nineveh* was fent,
In Sackcloth clad they generally repent.
The King he leaves his lofty fplended Throne,
In Afhes fets before the LORD to mourn,
Shall Gofpel Sinners be more vile than they,
In Judgment then will rife old *Nineveh*.

The *Sodomites* and the *Gomorians* too,
Will have a Doom lefs fearful far than you.
O tell it not in Streets of *Afkelon*,
Left vile *Philiftines* vaunt themfelves thereon,
Left Daughters of uncircumcis'd do noies,
And at fuch Tidings mightily rejoice.
Since GOD has fent his lovely *Whitefield* here,
And bleffed *Tennent*, O do not, do not dare,
To flight the Tenders of his wonderous Grace,
Who faves poor Souls in wife and fovereign Ways,
If on a Bed of Languifhing you lay,
For fome good Surgeon how you'd feek and pray ?
You'd fpare no Coft fo you cou'd but obtain
Eafe from Diftrefs and Freedom from your Pain.
How can you then find in your Hearts to flight
Your Souls Phyficians---- who ftudy Day and Night,
To find a Balfom for your bleeding Soul,
And precious Remedies to make them whole.
The poor, when fick, can fcarce a Doctor have
For want of Money which they often crave.
But Soul Remedies are offer'd on free Coft
That you'll not take them, grieves your Teachers moft.
Poor wounded Souls, O do not then delay ;
To Soul Phyficians hafte O hafte away.
As foon as fick, apply immediately,
Don't perifh while you have Relief fo nigh.
The Day of Grace may foon a Period have,
And then in vain you'll call, you'll cry and crave,
But all in vain : To Hell to Hell you muft
And be for Ever, Ever, Ever curft.
And now he's gone, the heavenly Man is gone,
Blefs GOD for faithful Shepherds of our own :
Who loudly call, and fain would Souls allure,
To make their Calling and Election fure.
O prize them, and rejoice in their fweet Light,
Who're glad to ferve your Souls by Day or Night.
They're glad to fhow the wandering Soul his Way,
From thofe dark Shades, to an eternal Day.
Follow your Shepherds they'll land you fafe afhore,
On Emanuel's Land, though Men and Devils roar.

F I N I S.

Vote in relation of Small Pox.

Boston ff.

At a Meeting of the Select-Men *February* 21. 1746.

WHEREAS the Small Pox for fome Time paft hath prevail'd in the neighbouring Governments, and ftill continues there, and Perfons coming from thofe Places, as alfo many others in this Province do not conform to the Laws made relating to that Diftemper : Therefore

Voted, That the Act of this Province made in the fixteenth Year of his prefent Majefty's Reign Intitled *An Act to prevent the fpreading of the Small-Pox and other infectious Sicknefs, and to prevent the concealing of the fame* ; be forthwith printed and pofted up that none may plead Ignorance, *Viz.*

An Act to prevent the fpreading of the Small-Pox and other infectious Sicknefs, and to prevent the concealing of the fame.

WHEREAS the Inhabitants of fundry Towns in this Province are often expofed to the Infection of the Small-Pox and other malignant contagious Diftempers, by Perfons coming from the neighbouring Governments vifited with fuch infectious Sicknefs, and by Goods transported hither that carry Infection with them :

Be it therefore enacted by the Governour, Council and House of Representatives, That any Perfon or Perfons coming from any Place (in either of the neighbouring Colonies or Provinces) where the Small-Pox or other malignant infectious Diftemper is prevailing, into any Town within this Province, who fhall not within the Space of two Hours from their firft coming, or from the Time they fhall firft be informed of their Duty by Law in this Particular, give Notice to one or more of the Select-Men or Town Clerk of fuch Town of their coming thither, and of the Place from whence they came, fhall forfeit and pay the Sum of *twenty Pounds* ; and if any Perfon or Perfons coming into any Town of this Province from any fuch Place vifited with the Small-Pox or other infectious Sicknefs, fhall not within the Space of two Hours (after Warning given him or them for that Purpofe by the Select-Men of fuch Town) depart out of this Province, in fuch Cafe it fhall and may be lawful for any Juftice of the Peace of fuch County by Warrant directed to a Conftable or other proper Officer to caufe fuch Perfon or Perfons to be removed (with any their Goods that may probably give Infection) unto the Colony or Government from whence they came, and any Perfon removed by Warrant as aforefaid, who (during the Prevalency of fuch Diftemper) fhall prefume to return into any Town of this Province without Liberty firft obtained from fuch Juftice, or from the Select-Men of fuch Town, fhall forfeit and pay the Sum of *One Hundred Pounds.*

And be it further enacted, That any Inhabitant of this Province who fhall entertin in his Houfe any Perfon warned to depart as aforefaid by the Space of two Hours after Notice given him or her by one or more of the Select-Men of fuch Warning, fhall forfeit and pay the Sum of *twenty Pounds.*

And be it further enacted, That it fhall and may be lawful for the Select-Men of any Town or Towns near to or bordering on either of the neighbouring Governments, to appoint (by Writing under their Hands) fome meet Perfon or Perfons to attend at Ferries or other Places by or over which Paffengers and Travellers coming from fuch infected Places may pafs or be tranfported ; which Perfon or Perfons fo appointed fhall have Power to examine fuch Paffengers and Travellers as they may fufpect to bring Infection with them, and (if Need be) to hinder and reftrain them from travelling, 'till licenced thereto by a Juftice of the Peace within fuch County, or by the Select-Men of the Town into which fuch Perfon or Perfons fhall come ; and any Paffenger who coming from fuch infected Place fhall (without Licence as aforefaid)

prefume to travel or abide in this Province after they fhall have been cautioned and admonifhed (by the Perfon or Perfons appointed as aforefaid) to depart, fhall forfeit and pay the Sum of *twenty Pounds,* and be removed thence by Warrant as aforefaid.

The feveral Forfeitures arifing by Virtue of this Act, to be one Moiety to and for the Ufe of the Town where the Offence fhall be committed, the other Moiety to him or them who fhall inform and fue for the fame in any of His Majefty's Courts of Record within this Province.

And be it further enacted, That from and after the Publication of this Act, when any Perfon is vifited with the Small Pox in any Town of this Province, immediately upon Knowledge thereof, the Head of the Family in which fuch Perfon is fick, fhall acquaint the Select-Men of the Town therewith, and alfo hang out on a Pole at leaft fix Feet in length, a red Cloth not under one Yard long and half a Yard wide, from the moft publick Part of the infected Houfe, the faid Sign thus to continue 'till the Houfe in the Judgment of the Select-Men is throughly aired and cleanfed, upon Penalty of forfeiting and paying the Sum of *fifty Pounds* for each Offence, one Half for the Informer, and the other Half for the Ufe of the Poor of the Town where fuch Offence fhall be committed, to be fued for and recovered by the Treafurer of the Town, or the Informer by Action, Bill, Plaint or Information in any of His Majefty's Courts of Record, and if the Party be unable or refufes to pay fuch Fine, then to be punifhed by Whipping, not exceeding thirty Stripes.

And be it further enacted, That when the Small Pox is in any Town of this Province, and any Perfon in faid Town (not having had the fame) fhall then be taken fick, and any peftulous Eruptions appear, the Head of that Family wherein fuch Perfon is, fhall immediately acquaint one or more of the Select-Men of the Town therewith (that fo the faid Select-Men may give Directions therein) upon Penalty of forfeiting the Sum of *fifty Pounds,* to be recovered and applied for the Ufes aforefaid, the whole Charge to be born by the Perfon thus vifited, if able to defrey the fame, but if in the Judgment of the Select-Men of the Town fuch Perfon is indigent and unable, then the faid Charge to be born by the Town whereto he or fhe belongs.

Provided always, That this Act fhall not be underftood to extend to Perfons in any Town where more than twenty Families are known to be vifited with the Small Pox at one and the fame Time.

This Act to continue and be in Force for the Space of feven Years, and no longer.

[*This Act was Publifhed* January 17. 1742.]

And all Perfons guilty of the Breach of the abovefaid Law, are hereby notified that the Select-Men are determin'd to profecute them for the fame.

By Order of the Select-Men,

Ezekiel Goldthwait, Town Clerk.

Bofton, February 21ft 1746.

*I*T having been reported for feveral Days that the Small-Pox was in the Town of Bofton : The Publick are hereby informed, that Yefterday His Majefty's Juftices of the Peace, the Select-Men and Overfeers of the Poor, within faid Town, on a general Vifitation of the Inhabitants did not find any Perfon fick of the *Small-Pox,* or that had any Symptoms of that Diftemper.

By Order of the Select-Men,

Ezekiel Goldthwait, Town Clerk.

An exact TABLE to bring Old Tenor into Lawful Money. Also a TABLE to know the Value of Piſtoles, Guineas, Johannes, and double Johannes, Moydores, Engliſh Crowns, Half-Crowns, Shillings, and Copper Half-Pence, at the Rate of Dollars at *Six Shillings* a Piece, at which invariable Value they are fixed by a late Act of this Government. The Act to be in Force from and after the 31ſt of *March* 1750.

INASMUCH as by an Act of this Province, Entitled, *An Act for drawing in the Bills of Credit of the ſeveral Denominations, which have at any Time been iſſued by this Government, and are ſtill outſtanding, and for aſcertaining the Rate of Coined Silver in this Province,* among other Things it is Enacted, That from and after the 31ſt of *March* 1750, that *Forty-five Shillings* of the Old Tenor, and *Eleven Shillings* and *three Pence* of the new and middle Tenor, ſhall be equal to one Piece of Eight, and ſhall be exchanged by the Treaſurer, with the Poſſeſſor or Poſſeſſors accordingly.

And whereas it is further Enacted, That all Bargains, Contracts, Debts and Dues whatſoever, which ſhall be contracted after the ſaid 31ſt of *March*, ſhall be underſtood to be in Silver at *Six Shillings* and *eight Pence* per Ounce; and all Spaniſh Mill'd Pieces of Eight ſhall be taken and paid at the Rate of *Six Shillings* a Piece and no more, on the Penalty of *Fifty Pounds* lawful Money——And all Perſons whatſoever are thereby required to conform their Books and Accounts according to ſaid Regulation: And any Books and Accounts, which ſhall not be made to conform to ſaid Regulation, will not be admitted by ſaid Act to be produced in Evidence, for the Recovery of any Debt in any of his Majeſty's Courts within this Province;

Therefore, That all Perſons may with Eaſe conform their Books and Accounts to the above Regulation, by bringing their Old Tenor Debts into lawful Money, according to the Intent and Deſign of ſaid Act, the following TABLE is offered to the Publick, by the Help of which even thoſe that are not well acquainted with Figures, may eaſily bring any Sum of Money of the Old Tenor into the eſtabliſhed Currency of the Year 1750.

And whereas it is highly probable that we ſhall, not only have Mill'd Dollars paſſing as a Currency among us after the 31ſt of *March* aforeſaid, but other Species of Money, as *Engliſh Crowns, Guineas, Piſtoles,* &c. And inaſmuch as by the Act aforeſaid, the Value of no Money is fixed, but that of Mill'd Pieces of Eight, therefore another TABLE is here preſented to ſhew as near as poſſible what Proportion Guineas, Piſtoles, &c. bear to Dollars at *Six Shillings,* that ſo all Perſons may know at what Rate to take and paſs them in their Trade and Buſineſs, or exchange them for Dollars.

Nothing is here ſaid concerning the Rate that Engliſh *Copper Half-Pence* muſt paſs at, by Reaſon that the Government being poſſeſſed of ſo large a Quantity, will no Doubt fix their Value: But with humble Submiſſion, ſhould they put the Value of a *Penny* on an Engliſh *Half-Penny* (as it is thought by ſome they will) there is great Danger that it will be attended with *very fatal Conſequences.* For any one, the leaſt acquainted with Trade and Buſineſs, muſt be convinced that in a few Years we ſhall not have a ſingle Dollar in the Province, but ſhall have *Copper* ſubſtituted in the Room of *Silver,* with this additional Misfortune, that we ſhall ſink one Third Part of the Sterling Value of the original Grant made by His Majeſty to this Province: For at preſent no Trade is ſo advantageous as ſhipping off Dollars, either to *New York, Philadelphia,* or *Great-Britain,* and importing *Half-Pence* for Returns, provided thoſe Half-Pence are worth here a Penny Lawful Money. But ſhould the Government exchange them, and enact that others ſhould take them in a juſt Proportion with Dollars, then the true Value of them which is annexed to the Table to know the Value of coin'd Gold, &c. may be of Service.

Old Tenor £. s. d.	Lawful Money £. s. d.	Old Tenor £.	Lawful Money £. s. d.	Old Tenor £.	Lawful Money £. s. d.	A Table to know what muſt be allowed for other Species of Money
1 3	is 2	32 is	4 5 4	78 is	10 8	beſides Dollars; accounting Dollars at *Six Shillings* a Piece lawful Money,
2 6	4	33	4 8	79	10 10 8	and ſuppoſing they are worth but
3 9	6	34	4 10 8	80	10 13 4	*Four Shillings and Six Pence* a Piece
5	8	35	4 13 4	81	10 16	Sterling: *Viz.*
6 3	10	36	4 16 8	82	10 18 8	A Piſtole is worth 22ſ
7 6	1	37	4 18 8	83	11 1 4	A Guinea 28ſ
8 9	1 2	38	5 1 4	84	11 4	A Moydore 36ſ
10	1 4	39	5 4	85	11 6 8	A 36ſ Sterling Piece 48ſ
11 3	1 6	40	5 6 8	86	11 9 4	A *l.*3 12ſ Sterl. Piece *l.*4 16ſ
12 6	1 8	41	5 9 4	87	11 12	An Engliſh Crown 6ſ 8d
13 9	1 10	42	5 12	88	11 14 8	An Half Crown 3ſ 4d
15	2	43	5 14 8	89	11 17 4	An Engliſh Shilling 1ſ 4d
16 3	2 2	44	5 17 4	90	12	An Engliſh Six Pence 8d
17 6	2 4	45	6	91	12 2 8	18 Copper Half Pence 12d
18 9	2 6	46	6 2 8	92	12 5 4	15 Ditto 10d
1	2 8	47	6 5 4	93	12 8	12 Ditto 8d
2	5 4	48	6 8	94	12 10 8	9 Ditto 6d
3	8	49	6 10 8	95	12 13 4	6 Ditto 4d
4	10 8	50	6 13 4	96	12 16	3 Ditto 2d
5	13 4	51	6 16	97	12 18 8	1 Ditto and 1 Farthing 1d
6	16	52	6 18 8	98	13 1 4	Admitting that Dollars are worth
7	18 8	53	7 1 4	99	13 4	*Four Shillings and Seven Pence Half*
8	1 1 4	54	7 4	100	13 6 8	*Penny* Sterling, as is ſometimes the
9	1 4	55	7 6 8	200	26 13 4	Caſe, then the following Table may
10	1 6 8	56	7 9 4	300	40	be of Uſe: *Viz.*
11	1 9 4	57	7 12	400	53 6 8	A Piſtole is worth but 21ſ 6d
12	1 12	58	7 14 8	500	66 13 4	A Guinea 27ſ 4d
13	1 14 8	59	7 17 4	600	80	A Moydore 35ſ 1d
14	1 17 4	60	8	700	93 6 8	A 36ſ Sterling Piece 46ſ 10d
15	2	61	8 2 8	800	106 13 4	A *l.*3 12ſ Piece *l.*4 13ſ 8d
16	2 2 8	62	8 5 4	900	120	An Engliſh Crown 6ſ 6d
17	2 5 4	63	8 8	1000	133 6 8	An Half Crown 3ſ 3d
18	2 8	64	8 10 8			An Engliſh Shilling 15d half Pen.
19	2 10 8	65	8 13 4	7447	992 18 8	An Engliſh Six Pence 7d 3 Farth.
20	2 13 4	66	8 16	2507	334 13 4	
21	2 16	67	8 18 8	503 10 0	67 2 8	
22	2 18 8	68	9 1 4			
23	3 1 4	69	9 4	10457 10 0	1394 6 8	
24	3 4	70	9 6 8			BOSTON, Jan. 1. 1749, 50.
25	3 6 8	71	9 9 4		7½	
26	3 9 4	72	9 12		9760 6 8	*N. B. Seven Pence half Penny old*
27	3 12	73	9 14 8		697 3 4	*Tenor, is One Penny lawful Money.*
28	3 14 8	74	9 17 4			
29	3 17 4	75	10	£. 10457 10 0		
30	4	76	10 2 8			
31	4 2 8	77	10 5 4			
503 10 0	67 2 8	2507	334 5 4			

BOSTON, Printed and Sold by *Rogers* and *Fowle* in Queen-Street. 1750.

VERSES

Occasioned by the EARTHQUAKES in the Month of *November*, 1755.

By *Jeremiah Newland*.

O God of Mercy thou art good,
  Thou Care for us did take,
When by thy Hand thou did Command,
  the Earth and Sea to shake.

What Heart so hard that can't be jarr'd,
  when thou the Earth doth shake :
O Lord what Eye can then be dry,
  in terrible EARTHQUAKE.

Thy terrible Hand is on the Land,
  by bloody War and Death ;
It is because we broke thy Laws,
  that thou didst shake the Earth.

Is ten good Men in each Town then ?
  because our Towns are spar'd !
Bless God that they have made a Way,
  that God might us Regard.

God looked strait in *Sodom*'s Gate,
  but ten good Men were not ;
But yet we see he did agree,
  with *Abraham* and *Lot*.

God would be just if he had thrust
  us in the gaping Ground ;
When we did shake by the Earthquake,
  clean is his guiltless Throne.

Come to the Lord with one Accord,
  and forth his Praises sound ;
For seeing he so kind to thee,
  and not to sink the Ground.

For by God's Hand, *New-England*
  was spared from much hurt ;
Tho' some buildings he down did fling,
  and lev'led with the durt.

We see O Lord, that thou hast jarr'd
  most every Habitation ;
By that we know, thou'rt strong enough
  to sink the whole Creation.

Let every Tongue, both Old and Young,
  and every Nation praise
The God of Host and Holy Ghost,
  for Christ, his Saints will raise.

By rending Rocks and by Earth Shocks,
  graves open by Direction ;
The Saints arose and that to see
  our Saviour's Crucifixion.

The old must dye, you can't deny,
  the young he doth command ;
The middle-age when death engage,
  though strong, yet can't withstand.

What Age or Sect will then neglect,
  a Pardon for to seek ;
When God hath told the Young and Old
  as plain as Words can speak.

Then do not say old People may
  be e'er too old for Death ;
For it is sent in a Moment,
  'twill snatch away their Breath.

Then O young Man, don't say you can
  your self from Death deliver ;
Your Fathers surely now are dead ;
  Can Prophets live for ever ?

O how can we who sinners be
  expect a dwelling here ?
When God doth call, both great and small
  to Judgment must appear.

What shall I say, of Youth, I pray ;
  O ! Can they Conquer Death ?

For when it goes with deadly Blows,
  'twill strike away their Breath.

There comes a Day, the Scriptures say,
  when every Tribe must meet,
To see the Judge of Quick and Dead,
  at his Tribunal Seat.

O what a Day the Scriptures say,
  the EARTHQUAKE doth foretell ;
O turn to God ; lest by his Rod,
  he cast thee down to Hell.

Mountains like Rams & Hills like Lambs,
  they Skipping till declin'd ;
The Rocks then clifts so fast,
  no Shelter could I find.

Where shall I run for Shelter then,
  but unto Christ my Rock,
And pray that he will Shelter me
  amongst his chosen Flock.

That I might stand at Christ's right Hand
  the Day of Great Assize ;
And sing most sweet and fly to meet,
  my Jesus in the Skies.

O God of Grace shine on my Face,
  The Beams of Glory shine ;
That I might Sing to Christ my King,
  when he says I am thine.

Then do attend, O Lord and send,
  thy *Jonah* unto us ;
That he may Preach and ever Teach,
  and take away the Curse.

Then give us Space and give us Grace,
  that we may give thee praise ;
We know not but we shall be sunk
  in less than forty Days.

Blessed be God that I have trod
  the Earth that might have fell ;
For it is he that maketh me,
  in Safety for to dwell.

Lord guide our Way in every Day,
  and give us Hearts of Prayer ;
That so we may not go the Way
  into the Devil's Snare.

Pardon the Sin we was born in,
  that's the Original ;
And keep us from the Way that goes
  into the Gate of Hell.

And let O Lord, thy Spirit guard,
  our Bodies Day and Night ;
Thou might most justly cut us off,
  and cast us out of Sight.

The Lord hath told he can't behold,
  the Face of a Deceiver ;
But he delights and so invites
  the penitent Believer.

If you deceive and can't believe,
  you surely then shall feel,
The Weight of Wrath the Curse for Sloth,
  that God will then reveal.

Believe I pray what God did say,
  the Words are of his Mouth ;
For what he said he'll make it good,
  he sware it with an Oath.

Blest three in one, Father and Son,
  the Holy Ghost, thy Spirit ;
Because that he's the way to thee,
  tho' he's not our Merit.

And O therefore we must adore
  our *Jesus* for his Merit ;
For 'tis by the Eternal three,
  the Father, Son and Spirit.

And pray that he would take from thee,
  if it should be his Will ;
That heavy Judgment which he sent,
  and send us Mercies still.

Let every knee, Lord bow to thee,
  and every Tongue confess ;
That thou art Lord, and by thy Word,
  dost Judge in Righteousness.

Take away Sin that cursed thing,
  in which we did delight :
Make us a People near to God,
  and form our Spirits Right.

Let us in Time, whilst we have Prime,
  for to be getting Store :
Whilst in our Health, for to get Wealth,
  that last for ever more.

Dont covet more, nor cheat the Poor,
  dont scorn thy Enemies ;
For what you get, by false deceit,
  wisdom calls vanity.

If you be great in your Estate,
  'twill lead you in a snare ;
The little that the poor Man gets
  is Blessed, tho' he's Poor.

Dont think that we more Righteous be,
  because we did Escape :
Altho' some Towns were totter'd down,
  when as the Earth did Shake.

Let us not stand at Babels hand,
  Let's not a Tower have ;
Lest we come down unto the Ground,
  and loose our Language then.

O *Jesus* ! send Angels to tend
  and fetch us home from far ;
That we may run to that bright Sun
  which is the Morning Star.

And so O Lord, send forth thy word,
  into our inward Parts :
And write a Law of Gratitude,
  and set it on our Hearts.

Don't when you look despise these Lines,
  tho' you may the inditer,
Because my Tongue, is not like one
  that is a ready Writer.

And do not look upon these Lines,
  to make a merry Story ;
But when you read do then proceed,
  to give to God the Glory.

Then let us join with one Design,
  our thankful Voices raise ;
And sing to him that dy'd for Sin,
  who's worthy of our Praise.

For in his Face shines Beams of Grace,
  a Pardon hath in Store ;
He dy'd for Sin and rose again,
  who lives for Evermore.

And don't I say forget that Day,
  the Eighteenth of *November* ;
On Tuesday Morn the Lord did warn,
  let us always remember.

F I N I S.

The Agonies of a Soul departing out of Time into Eternity.

A few Lines occasioned by the untimely End of *John Harrington*,
Who is to be Executed at *Cambridge* this Day, being the 17th of *March*, 1757, for the
Murder of *Paul Learnard*, the 1st of *September* last.

1.
AND is my Life already past ?
    Too early fled away ;
And will these Moments be my last ?
    And must I die to day ?

2.
Death ! nameless Horrors, swell the sound,
    And o'er my Conscience roll :
I feel his Stings, O how they wound !
    And terrify my Soul.

3.
Will no kind Being interpose,
    And mitigate the Smart ;
No friendly Hand allay the Woes,
    That terrify my Heart.

4.
See ! all astonish'd at my Crime
    My hated Presence fly ;
Nor would one Hour of Life redeem,
    Or pity, though I die.

5.
Justice arrouz'd ; puts on her Frown,
    In me her Terrors meet :
Her killing Accents melt me down ;
    I shudder at her Feet.

6.
Go Murd'rous Wretch, deep-drench'd in Gore ;
    With human Blood prophan'd ;
Thy Life we must admit no more,
    A Burthen to the Land.

7.
Thy harden'd Soul to Mercy steel'd,
    Unpitying dealt the Blow :
Thy Rage Remorseless, plain reveal'd,
    The unrelenting Foe.

8.
Go Wretch, devoted to the Grave,
    Let Death for Death atone ;
Go learn what Agonies you gave,
    And Groan for every Groan.

9.
Thus from the Earth indignant hurl'd,
    Ah ! whither shall I roam ;
What other distant unknown World
    Shall be my future Home ?

10.
Shall I with all my horrid Guilt
    To God exalt my Prayer ?
Will he forgive the Blood I've spilt,
    And shroud a Murd'rer there.

11.
O save me gracious King of Heaven,
    Enthron'd in State above ;
Be all my mighty Sins forgiv'n,
    Redeem me by thy Love.

12.
For ev'ry Stain, I'll drop a Tear,
    And at thy Feet I'll fall ;
Kind Mercy, smile away my Fear,
    And Pardon me for all.

13.
Tho' I have multiply'd my Crimes,
    So numerous and so great,
And sinn'd ten thousand thousand times,
    And dar'd Almighty hate.

14.
With thy Benevolence divine,
    A prostrate Wretch survey ;
And be the glorious Blessing thine,
    To open glorious Day.

15.
Dispell the Mists that cloud my Mind,
    And all my Pangs abate ;
Give this Example to Mankind,
    Of Love and Grace compleat.

16.
Submissive to thy gracious Will,
    I'll then resign my Breath ;
Earth's just Demands, I'll glad fulfill,
    And even smile in Death.

17.
Thy blissful Presence be my Joy,
    And all my Gloom dispell :
This shall the Sting of Death destroy,
    And sooth the Pangs of Hell.

18.
Then shall this Truth be ever known,
    While God sustains this Frame ;
In me his boundless Mercy shone,
    And Goodness is his Name.

No. 19

By His Excellency

THOMAS POWNALL, Esq;

Captain-General and Governor in Chief, in and over His Majesty's Province of the *Massachusetts-Bay* in *New-England*, and Vice-Admiral of the same, *&c.*

A PROCLAMATION.

HAVING on the Twenty-third Day of *March* last, issued my Proclamation for Encouraging the Inlistment of Seven Thousand Men into His Majesty's Service for a general Invasion of *Canada* ; therein setting forth, That this Government had promised unto each able-bodied effective Man, who should voluntarily inlist into said Service before the Fifteenth Day of *April* Instant, and pass Muster, a Bounty of FOUR POUNDS, and a good Blanket : And to every Non-commission Officer and private Soldier that should voluntarily inlist in the Service aforesaid, and actually proceed in it, the Sum of TEN POUNDS, to be paid to every such Person on his Return ; or to his Executors or Administrators in Case he die in the Service, provided the Government of *Canada* shall by the proposed Expedition be reduced to a Subjection to His Majesty's Arms : And had likewise made an Establishment for the Wages of each private Centinel at the Rate of *Thirty-six Shillings* per Month : And had further made Provision for advanc   to each private Man from the Time of his Inlistment, *six Pence* Sterling per Day for his Subsistence, until he shall arrive at such Place where he receives the King's Provisions ;

AND WHEREAS the Great and General Court, in order to compleat the Levy of said Men, have lengthened out the Time for their Inlistment upon the same Bounty until the Second Day of *May* next ;

I Do hereby promise in behalf of this His Majesty's Province of the *Massachusetts-Bay*, that there shall be a full Compliance with such Engagement ; and that all such Persons who shall inlist as aforesaid, shall be further intitled to all other Priviledges and Advantages set forth in the forementioned Proclamation ;---provided, said Men shall inlist at or before Four of the Clock in the Afternoon of the said Second Day of *May* : After which Time all such able-bodied Men as are fit for the Service, and who are not by Law exempted, will be liable to an Impress, in Consequence of the same Order of the Great and General Court, and will not be intitled to the Bounty or Privileges engaged to such as shall voluntarily inlist before.

GIVEN at Boston, *the Twenty-second Day of* April, 1758. *in the Thirty-first Year of the Reign of our Sovereign Lord* GEORGE *the Second, by the Grace of* GOD *of* Great-Britain, France *and* Ireland, *King, Defender of the Faith, &c.*

By His Excellency's Command,
  A. Oliver, Secr.

T. Pownall.

GOD Save the KING.

BOSTON : Printed by *John Draper*, Printer to His Excellency the Governor and the Honorable His Majesty's Council, M,DCC,LVIII.

An Account of the Fire at *Harvard-College,*
in *Cambridge;* with the Loſs ſuſtained thereby.

CAMBRIDGE, JAN. 25. 1764.

LAST night HARVARD COLLEGE, ſuffered the moſt ruinous loſs it ever met with ſince its foundation. In the middle of a very tempeſtuous night, a ſevere cold ſtorm of ſnow attended with high wind, we were awaked by the alarm of fire. *Harvard* Hall, the only one of our ancient buildings which ſtill remained,* and the repoſitory of our moſt valuable treaſures, the public LIBRARY and Philoſophical APPARATUS, was ſeen in flames. As it was a time of vacation, in which the ſtudents were all diſperſed, not a ſingle perſon was left in any of the Colleges, except two or three in that part of *Maſſachuſetts* moſt diſtant from *Harvard,* where the fire could not be perceived till the whole ſurrounding air began to be illuminated by it : When it was diſcovered from the town, it had riſen to a degree of violence that defied all oppoſition. It is conjectured to have begun in a beam under the hearth in the library, where a fire had been kept for the uſe of the General Court, now reſiding and fitting here, by reaſon of the Small-Pox at Boſton : from thence it burſt out into the Library. The books eaſily ſubmitted to the fury of the flame, which with a rapid and irreſiſtable progreſs made its way into the Apparatus-Chamber, and ſpread thro' the whole building. In a very ſhort time, this venerable Monument of the Piety of our Anceſtors was turn'd into an heap of ruins. The other Colleges, *Stoughton*-Hall and *Maſſachuſetts*-Hall, were in the utmoſt hazard of ſharing the ſame fate. The wind driving the flaming cinders directly upon their roofs, they blazed out ſeveral times in different places ; nor could they have been ſaved by all the help the Town could afford, had it not been for the aſſiſtance of the Gentlemen of the General Court, among whom his Excellency the Governor was very active ; who, notwithſtanding the extreme rigor of the ſeaſon, exerted themſelves in ſupplying the town Engine with water, which they were obliged to fetch at laſt from a diſtance, two of the College pumps being then rendered uſeleſs. Even the new and beautiful *Hollis*-Hall, though it was on the windward ſide, hardly eſcaped. It ſtood ſo near to *Harvard,* that the flames actually ſeized it, and, if they had not been immediately ſuppreſſed, muſt have carried it.

But by the Bleſſing of God on the vigorous efforts of the aſſiſtants, the ruin was confined to *Harvard*-Hall ; and there, beſides the deſtruction of the private property of thoſe who had chambers in it, the public loſs is very great ; perhaps, irreparable. The Library and the Apparatus, which for many years had been growing, and were now judged to be the beſt furniſhed in America, are annihilated. But to give the public a more diſtinct idea of the loſs, we ſhall exhibit a ſummary view of the general contents of each, as far as we can, on a ſudden, recollect them.

Of the LIBRARY.

IT contained—The Holy Scriptures in almoſt all languages, with the moſt valuable Expoſitors and Commentators, ancient and modern :—The whole Library of the late learned Dr. Lightfoot, which at his death he bequeathed to this College, and contained the Targums, Talmuds, Rabbins, Polygot, and other valuable tracts relative to oriental literature, which is taught here : The library of the late eminent Dr. Theophilus Gale : —

—All the Fathers, Greek and Latin, in their beſt editions. — A great number of tracts in defence of revealed religion, wrote by the moſt maſterly hands, in the laſt and preſent century :— Sermons of the moſt celebrated Engliſh divines, both of the eſtabliſhed national church and proteſtant diſſenters :—Tracts upon all the branches of polemic divinity :—The donation of the venerable Society, for propagating the Goſpel in foreign parts, conſiſting of a great many volumes of tracts againſt Popery, publiſhed in the Reigns of Charles II. and James II. the Boylean lectures, and other the moſt eſteemed Engliſh ſermons :—A valuable collection of modern theological treatiſes, preſented by the Right Rev. Dr. Sherlock, late Lord Biſhop of London, the Rev. Dr. Hales, F. R. S. and Dr. Wilſon of London :—A vaſt number of philological tracts, containing the rudiments of almoſt all languages, ancient and modern :—The Hebrew, Greek and Roman antiquities.—The Greek and Roman Claſſics, preſented by the late excellent and catholic-ſpirited Biſhop Berkeley ; moſt of them the beſt editions :—A large Collection of Hiſtory and biographical tracts, ancient and modern.—Diſſertations on various Political ſubjects —The Tranſactions of the Royal Society, Academy of Sciences in France, Acta Eruditorum, Miſcellanea curioſa, the works of Boyle and Newton, with a great variety of other mathematical and philoſophical treatiſes.—A collection of the moſt approved Medical Authors, chiefly preſented by Mr. James, of the iſland of Jamaica ; to which Dr. Mead and other Gentlemen made very conſiderable additions : Alſo Anatomical cuts and two compleat Skeletons of different ſexes. This collection would have been very ſerviceable to a Profeſſor of Phyſic and Anatomy, when the revenues of the College ſhould have been ſufficient to ſubſiſt a gentleman in this character.—A few ancient and valuable Manuſcripts in different languages.—A pair of excellent new Globes of the largeſt ſize, preſented by Andrew Oliver, jun. Eſq;—A variety of Curioſities natural and artificial, both of American and foreign produce.—A font of Greek types (which, as we had not yet a printing-office, was repoſited in the library) preſented by our great benefactor the late worthy Thomas Hollis, Eſq; of London ; whoſe picture, as large as the life, and inſtitutions for two Profeſſorſhips and ten Scholarſhips, periſhed in the flames.——Some of the moſt conſiderable additions that had been made of late years to the library, came from other branches of this generous Family.

The library contained above five thouſand volumes, all which were conſumed, except a few books in the hands of the members of the houſe ; and two donations, one made by our late honorable Lieutenant Governor Dummer, to the value of 50 l. ſterling ; the other of 56 volumes, by the preſent worthy Thomas Hollis, Eſq; F. R. S. of London, to whom we have been annually obliged for valuable additions to our late library : Which donations, being but lately received, had not the proper boxes prepared for them ; and ſo eſcaped the general ruin.

As the library records are burnt, no doubt ſome valuable benefactions have been omitted in this account, which was drawn up only by memory.

Of the APPARATUS.

WHEN the late worthy THOMAS HOLLIS, Eſq; of London founded a Profeſſorſhip of Mathematics and Philoſophy in Harvard-College, he ſent a fine Apparatus for Experimental Philoſophy in its ſeveral Branches.

Under the head of *Mechanics,* there were machines for experiments of falling bodies, of the centre of gravity, and of centrifugal forces ;—the ſeveral mechanical powers, balances of different ſorts, levers, pullies, axes in peritrochio, wedges, compound engines ; with curious models of each in braſs.

In *Hydroſtatics,* very nice balances, jars and bottles of various ſizes fitted with braſs caps, veſſels for proving the grand hydroſtatic Paradox, ſiphons, glaſs models of pumps, hydroſtatic balance, &c.

In *Pneumatics,* there was a number of different tubes for the Torricellian experiment, a large double-barrell'd Air-pump, with a great variety of receivers of different ſizes and ſhapes ; ſyringes, exhauſting and condenſing ; Barometer, Thermometer ; —with many other articles.

In *Optics,* there were ſeveral ſorts of mirrors, concave, convex, cylindric ; Lenſes of different foci ; inſtruments for proving the fundamental law of refraction ; Priſms, with the whole apparatus for the Newtonian theory of light and colors; the camera obſcura, &c.

And a variety of inſtruments for miſcellaneous purpoſes.

THE following articles were afterwards ſent us by Mr. Thomas Hollis, Nephew to that generous Gentleman, viz. an Orrery, an armillary Sphere, and a box of Microſcopes ; all of exquiſite workmanſhip.

For *Aſtronomy,* we had before been ſupplied with Teleſcopes of different lengths ; one of 24 feet ; and a braſs Quadrant of 2 feet radius, carrying a Teleſcope of a greater length ; which formerly belonged to the celebrated Dr. Halley. We had alſo the moſt uſeful inſtruments for *Dialling* ;— and for *Surveying,* a braſs ſemicircle, with plain ſights and magnetic needle. Alſo, a curious Teleſcope, with a compleat apparatus for taking the difference of Level ; lately preſented by Chriſtopher Kilby, Eſq;

Many very valuable additions have of late years been made to this apparatus by ſeveral generous benefactors, whom i would be ingratitude not to commemorate here, as no veſtiges of their donations remain. We are under obligation to mention particularly, the late Sir Peter Warren, Knt. Sir Henry Frankland, Bart. Hon. Jonathan Belcher, Eſq; Lt. Governor of Nova-Scotia ; Thomas Hancock, Eſq; James Bowdoin, Eſq; Ezekiel Goldthwait, Eſq; John Hancock, A. M. of Boſton, and Mr. Gilbert Harriſon of London, Merchant. From theſe Gentlemen we received fine reflecting Teleſcopes of different magnifying powers ; and adapted to different obſervations ; Microſcopes of the ſeveral ſorts now in uſe ; Hadley's Quadrant fitted in a new manner ; a nice Variation Compaſs, and Dipping needle ; with inſtruments for the ſeveral magnetical and electrical experiments—all new, and of excellent workmanſhip.——ALL DESTROYED !

Cambridge, Jan. 26. 1764. As the General Aſſembly have this day chearfully and unanimouſly voted to rebuild *Harvard*-Hall, it encourages us to hope, that the LIBRARY and APPARATUS will alſo be repaired by the private munificence of thoſe who wiſh well to America, have a regard for New-England, and know the importance of literature to the Church and State.

◇◇◇◇◇◇◇◇◇◇◇◇◇◇◇◇◇◇◇◇◇◇◇◇◇◇◇◇◇◇

BOSTON: PRINTED BY R. AND S. DRAPER.
1764.

---

* *Harvard*-Hall, 42 feet broad, 97 long, and four ſtories high, was founded A. D. 1672.

ARTICLES
AGREED UPON
BY THE
Charitable IRISH SOCIETY, in Boston New-England,
FOR THE
Better MANAGEMENT of their CHARITY.

WHEREAS several gentlemen, merchants and others, of the Irish nation, residing in Boston aforesaid, from an affectionate and compassionate concern for any of the Irish nation, who shall be reduced by sickness, shipwreck, old age, or other infirmities, or unforeseen accidents, thought fit, on the seventeenth day of March, one thousand seven hundred and thirty seven, to form themselves into a charitable society, for the relief of such of their poor and indigent countrymen, as, by articles then by them agreed upon, may more fully appear; which have not fully answered the ends of so laudable an undertaking: The present society, at their annual meeting, held at Boston aforesaid, the tenth day of April, one thousand seven hundred and sixty four, did then and there choose a committee, to draw new articles, which have been read at their anual meeting, the ninth day of April, one thousand seven hundred and sixty five, and, *nemine contradicente*, voted to be observed *in future*, for the due regulation, and management of their charity; hoping and expecting, that all gentlemen, merchants and others of the Irish nation, or of Irish extraction, who are lovers of charity and their countrymen, will chearfully contribute according to their ability, to this undertaking.

I.
This charity is only to extend to and for the relief of such of the Irish nation, or of Irish extraction, who, by a majority of the society shall be deemed objects thereof, after having found them to be persons of good fame and repute.

II.
All Irish men, or of Irish extraction, being invited, and able to join in this charitable undertaking, and refusing the same, are for ever to be excluded the benefit thereof.

III
The admission of members shall be by consent of a majority of the society, at any of the meetings herein aftermentioned; and such person on his admission, shall pay the sum of six shillings at least. All donations or benefactions of the members, and other well disposed persons, shall be thankfully received, and entered in the society's books with the names of the donors.

IV.
No part of the stock shall remain above one year without being let to interest. When the interest thereof shall amount to twelve pound *per annum*, the same, or part thereof shall be given as charity, (provided application shall be made as in the next succeeding article) but not more than forty shillings to one person, except by a majority of votes of the members at an annual meeting, and then not to exceed four pounds to one person; and as the stock may increase, such by rules and orders may be made for the disposition thereof, as shall be agreed to by a majority of the voters at an annual meeting.

V.
All applications for relief, or charity, shall be by petition in writing, the allegations thereof to be in the knowledge of two or more of the members, and when charity shall be granted to any person or persons, he, she, or they shall acknowledge the receipt of the same, on the back of the petition so preferred.

VI.
The managers of this society shall be a president, vice-president, treasurer, secretary, three assistants, three keepers, with a servitor to attend the society. The managers to be natives of Ireland, or of Irish extraction, and inhabitants of Boston; and if any member shall not keep silence, when commanded thereto by the president or vice-president, he shall pay therefore, two shillings for each offence, which shall be applied towards defraying the expence of the then present meeting.

VII.
There shall be an annual meeting at Boston, the second Tuesday of April, at such place as the managers shall appoint, for the election of managers for the following year, and inspection of the former year's transactions; also five other meetings, on the second Tuesdays of June, August, October, December, and January, anually, for the admission of members, and collecting and disposing of charity; each member, at each meeting, shall pay six-pence, and to defray the expence of the meeting, three-pence.

VIII.
And that none may plead forgetfulness of these meetings, the servitor shall give the members notice of them, and be allowed for his trouble, as the members, at their annual meeting, shall think proper. The president or vice-president being in the chair, these articles are to be read, before any business shall be entered upon. All affairs to be determined by a majority of the then present voters: and if any member shall absent from any of the said meetings, without giving a reasonable excuse therefore, he shall pay one shilling for each time so absent: or if any member shall be in one years arrears successive, of their payments above expressed, he shall be debarred from voting untill such arrears are paid.

IX.
The secretary shall keep a fair journal of all votes, entries, donations, and other affairs of the society, and be allowed for the same, as the society at their annual meeting shall judge reasonable.

X.
No member shall be a borrower or surety. All bonds or notes payable to this society in time coming, shall have two sureties, payable to the president and vice president, or either of them, or either of their successors; and if any bond or note as aforesaid, shall not be paid in three months after demanded, the same shall be put in suit.

XI.
There shall be two hundred copies of the articles printed, at the expence of the society, and one of them delivered to each member, and one to every new member on his admission, which when dispersed, others shall be printed, if the society shall think convenient.

XII.
The keeper of the silver key, who shall be chosen always at an annual meeting, shall attend gentlemen and others, natives of Ireland, or of Irish extraction, residing in these parts, or transients, to acquaint them with this charitable design, and invite them to contribute, by the formality of shewing them said key, with the arms of Ireland therein; and if any do refuse, his or their name or names shall be made known to the next meeting.

Lastly. These articles are to be fairly wrote in the society's book, and the present members, with such as shall be hereafter admitted members, shall subscribe their names to them in said book, in token of their free consent to, and observation of them.

Success to the charitable Irish Society.

BOSTON: printed by W. M'ALPINE and J. FLEEMING. M,DCC,LXV.

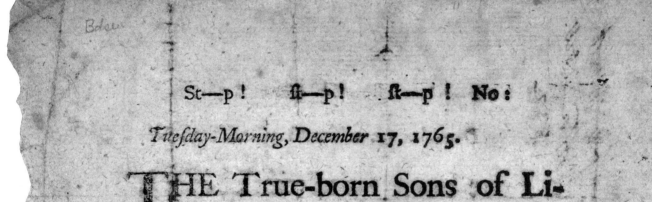

Advertisement.

THese are to give Notice to all Persons where these Papers shall come; that a Servant Man belonging to *Hannah Bosworth* of *Hull*; Whose Name is *Matthew Jones*: He is a *Taylor* by Trade, a Man of a middle stature, and pretty slender, about *twenty six* years of age, in good Apparel, a grey Caster Hat with a Clasp on it, a *Periwig of bright brown Hair*, in a close Coat & Breeches of a *brownish colour*, cloth Serge: Wolsted Stockins, and French Falls or Wooden heel'd Shoes: Ran away from his Mistriss the 22*d*. of *February* 1682. If any Person will secure this *Runaway* he shall be well satisfied for his pains; and whosoever shall bring him to *George Ellistone* Shop keeper in *Boston* shall have forty shillings in Money. There was a tall young man a *Bellows-maker* that worked in *Boston* in company with this *Taylor*, his Name is *Benjamin Smeed*.

March 6. 1683./4

No. 23

St—p! st—p! st—p! No:

Tuesday-Morning, December 17, 1765.

THE True-born Sons of Liberty, are desired to meet under LIBERTY-TREE, at XII o'Clock, THIS DAY, to hear the the public Resignation, under Oath, of ANDREW OLIVER, Esq; Distributor of Stamps for the Province of the *Massachusetts-Bay*.

A Resignation ? YES.

No. 24

THE
SPEECH
Of *Joseph T-sd-le*, Esq;

In the House of Representatives, June 1767, against the Bill then before the House, for preventing Stage Plays, *and other* Theatrical Entertainments.

Mr. S—k—r,

I AM well sensible that this subject would admit of a more extensive argument than I am able to advance, and merit the attention of this house; I shall therefore proceed to advance the little that lies upon my mind, in as laconick a manner as possible.

To proceed:

THEATRES have ever been countenanced in all free and civilized countries, and when plays are under good regulation, they are of admirable use, by carrying conviction into the mind with such irresistable force and energy, as to engage the whole faculties and powers of the soul in the cause of virtue; and the same faculties and powers will also be engaged in stifling vice in its first principles, or in its feeble beginnings; this is not too much to be attributed to a *Tragedy*:—What can be more engaging and instructive to the mind, than to see *CATO* represented dying for his country? What more soothing to the mind, after the fatigues of a day, than to see the representation of friends; the delicate and constant fathers; just children; tender, grateful and affectionate wives, faithful and obliging?——We ought to be very careful, and take care, that we drive not our youths from such noble amusements to the practice of something much more shameful and destructive, though perhaps more secret.——To make too severe laws is worse than not to make any; for what does it signify for us to make such laws as the people cannot, and will not observe; this will only tend to bring us into disrepute.—I dare say, that every member in this honorable house, have felt within themselves, times of disgust and uneasiness, even in the bosom of solitude as well as in the midst of the hurry of business, which required relaxation and amusement.—Need I say any thing more to impress upon this honorable assembly an opinion of an entertainment so pregnant with blessings?—Methinks I have said enough: But I have still something further,—I did not happen to be in the house the other day when the worthy gentleman from H———h spoke to the bill now before the house; but I heard that he spoke; I know the subject so well, and I have such an opinion of that gentleman's capacity, that I apprehend his argument was conclusive and unanswerable; if so, why do we pass this bill into an act, without getting over the objections that are made to it? I am at a loss to conceive. Do we do it to please the clergy?—Since I have been upon the stage of action, I have observed the clergy in general have made it their business to cry down all kinds of *Theatrical performances*; and it is not to be wondered at, since there is such a temporal interest depending upon their doing of it; if they had not done it, possibly there might by this time have risen up a set of people, that would have taken a more effectual method to improve the morals, and excite sentiments of virtue and religion, than what they have done:—A set of people I say, might have risen up, that would have taught the people in general, to have thought too wisely for the temporal interest of the clergy; but I dont say too wisely for the interest of Christ.—I have sometimes thought we seem to conduct as though we were about to set up and establish the kingdom of Christ by laws of our own making, which never can be done: It is not the warden law nor a *thousand white staff* men that will do it, nor prevent its being set up, where it is to be set up, neither will the law; for the kingdom of Christ takes its course like lightning, and is not to be directed by man, nor by the laws of men.—But to return more immediately to the point in question, and before I proceed any further, I shall acknowledge I never saw a *Play* acted in my life, therefore I am not so well able to set forth the beauty, the excellency, and the usefullness they are of to mankind in general, as though I had seen them acted; I have only had the advantage of reading them, and I dont imagine that my reading them has taught me to despise religion, virtue nor honesty; but rather taught me to be more in favour of them; all this is the effect it has had upon me—I should not have said so much was it not that I apprehend that the clergy were at the bottom of this motion; and I have no notion of having the general court rul'd by the clergy, while I have a seat here.—In antient times the clergy did as they pleas'd with the general court; then Quakers were hanged for witches; and they had a curious method of trying them, by binding them and throwing them into the water; if they could swim bound, they were taken out and hanged for witches, if not, they were only drowned;—this is some of the good fruits that arise by the general court's being rul'd and dictated by the clergy of old.——If any great inconveniency should arise to the Inabitants of *Boston*, on account of the insufficiency of the laws of this province, no doubt but they will petition the genaral court for another law to be made, and it will be time enough then for us to take this matter under our consideration.—And if any body should rise up between this and then to eclipse the glory of the clergy, it must be somebody that will take a more effectual method to excite sentiments of virtue and religion than what they have done, and set forth the odiousness of vice and immorality in a more striking manner than what they have done, otherwise their glory will not be eclipsed.—

No. 25

A MONUMENTAL INSCRIPTION

ON THE

Fifth of March.

Together with a few LINES

On the Enlargement of

EBENEZER RICHARDSON,

Convicted of MURDER.

AMERICANS!
BEAR IN REMEMBRANCE
The HORRID MASSACRE!
Perpetrated in King-ftreet, Boston,
New-England,
On the Evening of March the Fifth, 1770.
When FIVE of your fellow countrymen,
GRAY, MAVERICK, CALDWELL, ATTUCKS,
and CARR,
Lay wallowing in their Gore!
Being *bafely*, and moft *inhumanly*
MURDERED!
And SIX others badly WOUNDED!
By a Party of the XXIXth Regiment,
Under the command of Capt. Tho. Prefton.
REMEMBER!
That Two of the Murderers
Were convicted of MANSLAUGHTER!
By a Jury, of whom I fhall fay
NOTHING,
Branded in the hand!
And *difmiffed*,
The others were ACQUITTED,
And their Captain PENSIONED!
Alfo,
BEAR IN REMEMBRANCE
That on the 22d Day of February, 1770.
The infamous
EBENEZER RICHARDSON, Informer,
And tool to Minifterial hirelings,
Moft *barbaroufly*
MURDERED
CHRISTOPHER SEIDER,
An innocent youth!
Of which crime he was found guilty
By his Country
On Friday April 20th, 1770;
But remained *Unfentenced*
On Saturday the 22d Day of February, 1772.
When the GRAND INQUEST
For Suffolk county,
Were informed, at requeft,
By the Judges of the Superior Court,
That EBENEZER RICHARDSON'S *Cafe*
Then lay before his MAJESTY.
Therefore faid *Richardfon*
This day, MARCH FIFTH! 1772,
Remains UNHANGED!!!
Let THESE things be told to Pofterity!
And handed down
From Generation to Generation,
'Till Time fhall be no more!
Forever may AMERICA be preferved,
From weak and wicked monarchs,
Tyrannical Minifters,
Abandoned Governors,
Their Underlings and Hirelings!
And may the
Machinations of artful, *defigning* wretches,
Who would ENSLAVE THIS People,
Come to an end,
Let their NAMES and MEMORIES
Be buried in eternal oblivion,
And the PRESS,
For a *SCOURGE* to Tyrannical Rulers,
Remain FREE.

AWAKE my drowfy Thoughts! Awake my mufe!
Awake O earth, and tremble at the news!
In grand defiance to the laws of God,
The Guilty, Guilty murd'rer walks abroad.
That city mourns, (the cry comes from the ground,)
Where law and juftice never can be found:
Oh! fword of vengeance, fall thou on the race
Of thofe who hinder juftice from its place.
O MURD'RER! RICHARDSON! with their lateft breath
Millions will curfe you when you fleep in death!
Infernal horrors fure will fhake your foul
When o'er your head the awful thunders roll.
Earth cannot hide you, always will the cry
Of Murder! Murder! haunt you 'till you die!
To yonder grave! with trembling joints repair,
Remember, SEIDER's corps lies mould'ring there;
There drop a tear, and think what you have done!
Then judge how you can live beneath the Sun.
A PARDON may arrive! You laws defy,
But Heaven's laws will ftand when KINGS fhall die.
Oh! Wretched man! the monfter of the times,
You were not hung " by reafon of *old* Lines,"
Old Lines thrown by, 'twas then we were in hopes,
That you would foon be hung with *new made* Ropes;
But neither *Ropes nor Lines*, will fatisfiy
For SEIDER's blood! But GOD is ever nigh,
And guilty fouls will not unpunifh'd go
Tho' they're excus'd by judges here below!
You are enlarg'd but curfed is your fate
Tho' *Cufhing*'s eas'd you from the prifon gate
The --*Bridge* of *Tories*, *it* has borne you o'er
Yet you e'er long may meet with HELL's dark fhore.

A LIST of the Names of the PROVINCIALS who were Killed and Wounded in the late Engagement with His Majesty's Troops at *Concord*, &c.

KILLED.

Of *Lexington*.
* Mr. Robert Munroe,
* Mr. Jonas Parker,
* Mr. Samuel Hadley,
* Mr. Jonaⁿ Harrington,
* Mr. Caleb Harrington,
* Mr. Isaac Muzzy,
* Mr. John Brown,
Mr. John Raymond,
Mr. Nathaniel Wyman,
Mr. Jedediah Munroe.

Of *Menotomy*.
Mr. Jason Ruffel,
Mr. Jabez Wyman,
Mr. Jason Winship,

Of *Sudbury*.
Deacon Haynes,
Mr. ——— Reed.

Of *Concord*.
Capt. James Miles.

Of *Bedford*.
Capt. Jonathan Willson.

Of *Acton*.
Capt. Davis,
Mr. ——— Hofmer,
Mr. James Howard.

Of *Woburn*.
* Mr. Azael Porter,
Mr. Daniel Thompson.

Of *Charleftown*.
Mr. James Miller,
Capt. William Barber's Son.

Of *Brookline*.
Isaac Gardner, Esq;

Of *Cambridge*.
Mr. John Hicks,
Mr. Moses Richardson,
Mr. William Maffey.

Of *Medford*.
Mr. Henry Putnam.

Of *Lynn*.
Mr. Abednego Ramfdell,
Mr. Daniel Townfend,
Mr. William Flint,
Mr. Thomas Hadley.

Of *Danvers*.
Mr. Henry Jacobs,
Mr. Samuel Cook,
Mr. Ebenezer Goldthwait,
Mr. George Southwick,
Mr. Benjamin Daland, jun.
Mr. Jotham Webb,
Mr. Perley Putnam.

Of *Salem*.
Mr. Benjamin Peirce.

WOUNDED.

Of *Lexington*.
Mr. John Robbins,
Mr. John Tidd,
Mr. Solomon Peirce,
Mr. Thomas Winfhip,
Mr. Nathaniel Farmer,
Mr. Joseph Comee,
Mr. Ebenezer Munroe,
Mr. Francis Brown,
Prince Eafterbrooks,
(A Negro Man.

Of *Framingham*.
Mr. ——— Hemenway.

Of *Bedford*.
Mr. John Lane.

Of *Woburn*.
Mr. George Reed,
Mr. Jacob Bacon.

Of *Medford*.
Mr. William Polly.

Of *Lynn*.
Mr. Joshua Felt,
Mr. Timothy Munroe.

Of *Danvers*.
Mr. Nathan Putnam,
Mr. Dennis Wallis.

Of *Beverly*.
Mr. Nathaniel Cleaves.

MISSING.

Of *Menotomy*.
Mr. Samuel Froft,
Mr. Seth Ruffell.

Thofe diftinguifhed with this Mark [*] were killed by the firft Fire of the Regulars.

Boston: Edes and Gill, Sold in Queen-Street. [1775]

In Congress, *at* Watertown, *April* 30, 1775.

. Gentlemen,

THE barbarous Murders on our innocent Brethren on Wednesday the 19th Instant, has made it absolutely necessary that we immediately raise an Army to defend our Wives and our Children from the butchering Hands of an inhuman Soldiery, who, incensed at the Obstacles they met with in their bloody Progress, and enraged at being repulsed from the Field of Slaughter; will without the least doubt take the first Opportunity in their Power to ravage this devoted Country with Fire and Sword : We conjure you, therefore, by all that is dear, by all that is sacred, that you give all Assistance possible in forming an Army : Our all is at Stake, Death and Devastation are the certain Consequences of Delay, every Moment is infinitely precious, an Hour lost may deluge your Country in Blood, and entail perpetual Slavery upon the few of your Posterity, who may survive the Carnage. We beg and entreat, as you will answer it to your Country, to your own Consciences, and above all as you will answer to God himself, that you will hasten and encourage by all possible Means, the Inlistment of Men to form the Army, and send them forward to Head-Quarters, at Cambridge, with that Expedition, which the vast Importance and instant Urgency of the Affair demands.

JOSEPH WARREN, President, P. T.

In CONGRESS, July 4, 1776.

A DECLARATION

By the REPRESENTATIVES of the

UNITED STATES OF AMERICA,

In GENERAL CONGRESS ASSEMBLED.

WHEN in the Course of human Events, it becomes necessary for one People to diffolve the Political Bands which have connected them with another, and to affume among the Powers of the Earth, the feparate and equal Station to which the Laws of Nature and of Nature's God entitle them, a decent Refpect to the Opinions of Mankind requires that they fhould declare the Caufes which impel them to the feperation.

We hold thefe Truths to be felf-evident, that all Men are created equal, that they are endowed by their Creator with certain unalienable Rights, that among thefe are Life, Liberty, and the Purfuit of Happinefs.—That to fecure thefe Rights, Governments are inftituted among Men, deriving their juft Powers from the Confent of the Governed, that whenever any Form of Government becomes deftructive of thefe Ends, it is the Right of the People to alter or to abolifh it, and to inftitute new Government, laying its foundation on fuch Principles, and organizing its Powers in fuch Form, as to them fhall feem moft likely to effect their Safety and Happinefs. Prudence, indeed, will dictate that Governments long eftablifhed fhould not be changed for light and tranfient Caufes; and accordingly all Experience hath fhewn, that Mankind are more difpofed to fuffer, while Evils are fufferable, than to right themfelves by abolifhing the Forms to which they are accuftomed. But when a long Train of Abufes and Ufurpations, purfuing invariably the fame Object, evinces a Defign to reduce them under abfolute Defpotifm, it is their Right, it is their Duty, to throw off fuch Government, and to provide new Guards for their future Security. Such has been the patient Sufferance of thefe Colonies; and fuch is now the Neceffity which conftrains them to alter their former Syftems of Government. The Hiftory of the prefent King of Great-Britain is a Hiftory of repeated Injuries and Ufurpations, all having in direct Object the Eftablifhment of an abfolute Tyranny over thefe States. To prove this, let Facts be fubmitted to a candid World.

He has refufed his Affent to Laws, the moft wholefome and neceffary for the public Good.

He has forbidden his Governors to pafs Laws of immediate and preffing Importance, unlefs fufpended in their Operation till his Affent fhould be obtained; and when fo fufpended, he has utterly neglected to attend to them.

He has refufed to pafs other Laws for the Accommodation of large Diftricts of People, unlefs thofe People would relinquifh the Right of Reprefentation in the Legiflature, a Right ineftimable to them, and formidable to Tyrants only.

He has called together Legiflative Bodies at Places unufual, uncomfortable, and diftant from the Depofitory of their public Records, for the fole Purpofe of fatiguing them into Compliance with his Meafures.

He has diffolved Reprefentative Houfes repeatedly, for oppofing with manly Firmnefs his Invafions on the Rights of the People.

He has refufed for a long Time, after fuch Diffolutions, to caufe others to be elected; whereby the Legiflative Powers, incapable of Annihilation, have returned to the people at large for their exercife; the State remaining in the mean time expofed to all the Dangers of Invafion from without, and Convulfions within.

He has endeavoured to prevent the population of thefe States; for that Purpofe obftructing the Laws for Naturalization of Foreigners; refufing to pafs others to encourage their Migrations hither, and raifing the Conditions of new Appropriations of Lands.

He has obftructed the Adminiftration of Juftice, by refufing his Affent to Laws for eftablifhing Judiciary Powers.

He has made Judges dependent on his Will alone, for the Tenure of their Offices, and the Amount and Payment of their Salaries.

He has erected a multitude of new Offices, and fent hither Swarms of Officers to harrafs our People, and eat out their Subftance.

He has kept among us, in Times of Peace, Standing Armies, without the Confent of our Legiflatures.

He has affected to render the Military independent of and fuperior to the civil Power.

He has combined with others to fubject us to a Jurifdiction foreign to our Conftitution, and unacknowledged by our Laws; given his Affent to their Acts of pretended Legiflation:

For quartering large Bodies of armed Troops among us:

For protecting them, by a mock Trial, from Punifhment for any Murders which they fhould commit on the Inhabitants of thefe States:

For cutting off our Trade with all Parts of the World:

For impofing Taxes on us without our Confent:

For depriving us, in many Cafes, of the Benefits of Trial by Jury:

For tranfporting us beyond Seas to be tried for pretended Offences:

For abolifhing the free fyftem of Englifh Laws in a neighbouring Province, eftablifhing therein an arbitrary Government, and enlarging its Boundaries, fo as to render it at once an Example and fit Inftrument for introducing the fame abfolute Rule into thefe Colonies:

For taking away our Charters, abolifhing our moft valuable Laws, and altering fundamentally the Forms of our Governments:

For fufpending our own Legiflatures, and declaring themfelves invefted with Power to legiflate for us in all Cafes whatfoever.

He has abdicated Government here, by declaring us out of his Protection and waging War againft us.

He has plundered our Seas, ravaged our Coafts, burnt our Towns, and deftroyed the Lives of our People.

He is at this Time, tranfporting large Armies of foreign Mercenaries to compleat the Works of Death, Defolation and Tyranny, already begun with Circumftances of Cruelty and Perfidy fcarcely paralleled in the moft barbarous Ages, and totally unworthy the Head of a civilized Nation.

He has conftrained our fellow Citizens taken Captive on the high Seas to bear Arms againft their Country, to become the Executioners of their Friends and Brethren, or to fall themfelves by their Hands.

He has excited Domeftic Infurrections amongft us, and has endeavoured to bring on the Inhabitants of our Frontiers, the mercilefs Indian Savages, whofe known Rule of Warfare, is an undiftinguifhed Deftruction, of all Ages, Sexes and Conditions.

In every Stage of thefe Oppreffions we have petitioned for Redrefs, in the moft humble Terms: Our repeated Petitions have been anfwered only by repeated Injury. A Prince, whofe Character is thus marked by every Act which may define a Tyrant, is unfit to be the Ruler of a free People.

Nor have we been wanting in Attention to our Britifh Brethren. We have warned them from Time to Time of Attempts by their legiflature to extend an unwarrantable Jurifdiction over us. We have reminded them of the Circumftances of our Emigration and Settlement here. We have appealed to their native Juftice and Magnanimity, and we have conjured them by the Ties of our common Kindred to difavow thefe Ufurpations, which would inevitably interrupt our Connections and Correfpondence. They too have been deaf to the Voice of Juftice and of Confanguinity. We muft, therefore, acquiefce in the Neceffity which denounces our Separation, and hold them, as we hold the reft of Mankind, Enemies in War; in Peace, Friends.

We, therefore, the Reprefentatives of the UNITED STATES OF AMERICA, in GENERAL CONGRESS affembled, appealing to the Supreme Judge of the World for the Rectitude of our Intentions, do in the Name and by the Authority of the good People of thefe Colonies, folemnly Publifh and Declare, That thefe United Colonies are, and of Right ought to be, FREE AND INDEPENDENT STATES; that they are abfolved from all Allegiance to the Britifh Crown, and that all political Connection between them and the State of Great-Britain, is, and ought to be totally diffolved; and that as FREE AND INDEPENDENT STATES, they have full Power to levy War, conclude Peace, contract Alliances, eftablifh Commerce, and to do all other Acts and Things which INDEPENDENT STATES may of Right do. And for the Support of this Declaration, with a firm Reliance on the Protection of Divine Providence, we mutually pledge to each other our Lives, our Fortunes, and our facred Honor.

Signed by ORDER *and in* BEHALF *of the* CONGRESS,

JOHN HANCOCK, Prefident.

ATTEST.

CHARLES THOMPSON, Secretary.

AMERICA: BOSTON, Printed by JOHN GILL, and POWARS and WILLIS, in QUEEN-STREET.